TOTAL LOSS FARM

by Raymond Mungo

FAMOUS LONG AGO

TOTAL LOSS FARM

RAYMOND MUNGO

TOTAL LOSS FARM
A Year in the Life

E. P. DUTTON & CO., INC. | NEW YORK | 1970

SECOND PRINTING FEBRUARY 1971
Copyright © 1970 by Raymond Mungo
All rights reserved.
Printed in the U.S.A. by Vail-Ballou Press, Inc.

Published simultaneously in Canada by
Clarke, Irwin & Company Limited, Toronto and Vancouver

Library of Congress Catalog Card Number: 73-125905

SBN   0-525-22133-6

Sections of Part I originally appeared, in somewhat different form,
in the *Atlantic Monthly* (May, 1970) under the title
"If Mr. Thoreau Calls, Tell Him I've Left the Country."

Photos by Peter Simon

Drawing by Peter Gould

INVOCATION:
A Simple Song of the Life

Walking in Ireland with pack on my shoulders, Verandah and Sainte Helene by my side, I stooped to notice a beetle unhappily turned on its back, tiny legs thrashing the air for an impossible foothold. Put down the pack and, using a stray piece of hay, turned the little fellow aright and watched him walk away.

Just then decided I'd had enough and laid me down to die. "Fucking Ireland anyway, how do we get into these scenes?" Lived in mad commune in Scotland where sexual tension was enough to crack the ice around the Faeroe Islands. Honking seals and wild irritable swans and round-and-round sun cycle twenty-one hours a day. Helene saying, "I want to be nozzing" (she from Paris & bumming with us) "because nozzing is everyzing."

Unending warm sunshine made it impossible to die. Lying in the grass shading my eyes and dreaming of friends gone from me in the last year, and victims of war and uptightness all over the planet, and finally dreaming my own death: no easy slumber in Ireland green for this kid, but an explosion (source unknown) which sends my body in a million pieces flying all over the atmosphere.

"We who are living now," I dreamed, "are living the end of the movie."

Suddenly realized what comes after the end of the movie: the Life. Get out of your vinyl armchair and walk out into the street, leaving the flick behind, meet a stranger or two, fall in love, chase butterflies up to the orchard, father and mother your children, keep up your compost heap, feel the wind in your eyes. The Life is whatever you think it is. How it goes on and on!

The Life is a dream, the Life is a joke. Sometimes the joke's on us. The Life is a vision that came to me on the North wind. There's no use my wanting to be "nozzing," 'cause it ain't gonna happen. For better or worse, I'm here—so are you—so we might as well enjoy us.

After some years of lying still in the grass, I woke to the news that a stranger named Andy had offered us a ride to the Giant's Causeway —a series of stone steps leading from the Atlantic to the hills of the Antrim Coast. As we were going where the wind tilts, we accepted. Another adventure began on that wild causeway, and the little world of young Andy swallowed us up for a while. Till we moved on to the next place, and the next. If you want to survive, you gotta keep moving.

This book is a record of some of our moves, physical and spiritual. For every narrative, maxim, and realization in it, there are a million left out. Fortunately, the Life has been coming on so fast and strong that there's no time to record it all. We've absorbed our initial violent reaction against the society of our fathers, and are off on newer and more constructive adventures. In short, we are learning how to be alive again.

I am indebted to people all over the mother planet for assistance in creating this book: to just about everybody, I suppose. I hope this amuses you and eases your passage of time on the planet: if it doesn't, if it depresses you or makes you angry, I hope you will throw it away. World's got enough problems without me.

And, for Christ's sake, don't listen to all them. What do they know, anyway? Listen to your heart and goodwill, and feel your body, and you'll soon figure out what your natural and sacred role in this insane pageant really is. And where to go next.

1. FALL:

Another Week on the Concord and Merrimack Rivers

For Steve Lerner, wherever love may find him.

God help us,
refugees in winter dress,
Skating home on thin ice
from the Apocalypse.

—Verandah Porche

To one who habitually endeavors to contemplate the true state of things, the political state can hardly be said to have any existence whatever. It is unreal, incredible, and insignificant to him, and for him to endeavor to extract the truth from such lean material is like making sugar from linen rags, when sugar-cane may be had. Generally speaking, the political news, whether domestic or foreign, might be written to-day for the next ten years with sufficient accuracy. Most revolutions in society have not power to interest, still less alarm us; but tell me that our rivers are drying up, or the genus pine dying out in the country, and I might attend.

—Henry D. Thoreau,
A Week on the Concord and Merrimack Rivers

Friday: Portsmouth, N.H.

The farm in Vermont had fooled us, just as we hoped it would when we moved there in early '68; it had tricked even battle-scarred former youth militants into seeing the world as bright clusters of Day-Glo orange and red forest, rolling open meadows, sparkling brooks and streams. I had lived in industrial, eastern New England all my life, though, as well as worse places like New York and Washington, D.C., so I might have known better. But Vermont had blurred my memory, and when we finally left the farm for Portsmouth, I was all Thoreau and Frost, October up North, ain't life grand, all fresh and eager to begin rowing up the Concord and Merrimack rivers in the vanished footsteps of old Henry D. himself. Verandah Porche, queen of the Bay State Poets for Peace, packed the failing '59 VW and we went tearing down the mountain, kicking up good earth from the dirt road and barely slowing down for the 18th-century graveyard and all manner of wild animals now madly racing for shelter against the sharp winds of autumn in these hills. The frost was on the pumpkin, it was our second autumn together, and warm vibrations made the yellow farmhouse fairly glow in the dying daylight as we pointed east, over the Connecticut River, heading for our rendezvous with what *he* called "the placid current of our dreams." Knockout October day in 1969 in Vermont. All the trees had dropped acid.

The idea had come to me in a dream. It was one of those nights after Steve brought the Sunshine (wotta drug) when I'd wake up and sit bolt upright, alarmed at a sudden capacity, or *power,* I had acquired, to *see far.* I could see eternity in the vast darkness outside my window and inside my head, and I remembered feeling that way when but an infant. In my dream I was floating silently downstream in a birchbark canoe, speechless me watching vistas of bright New England autumn open up with each bend, slipping unnoticed between crimson mountains, blessing the warm sun by day and sleeping on beds of fresh leaves under a canary harvest moon by night. I was on the road to no special place, but no interstate highway with Savarinettes and Sunoco for this kid; in my dream, I was on a natural highway through the planet, the everlovin' me-sustainin' planet that never lets you down. Said Henry: "I have not yet put my foot through it."

It was the farm that had allowed me the luxury of this vision, for the farm had given me the insulation from America which the peace movement promised but cruelly denied. When we lived in Boston, Chicago, San Francisco, Washington (you name it, we lived there; some of us still live there), we dreamed of a New Age born of violent insurrection. We danced on the graves of war dead in Vietnam, every corpse was ammunition for Our Side; we set up a countergovernment down there in Washington, had marches, rallies and meetings; tried to fight fire with fire. Then Johnson resigned, yes, and the universities began to fall, the best and oldest ones first, and by God every 13-year-old in the suburbs was smoking dope and our numbers multiplying into the millions. But I woke up in the spring of 1968 and said, "This is not what I had in mind," because the movement had become my enemy; the movement was not flowers and doves and spontaneity, but another vicious system, the seed of a heartless bureaucracy, a minority Party vying for power rather than peace. It was then that we put away the schedule for the revolution, gathered together our dear ones and all our resources, and set off to Vermont in search of the New Age.

The New Age we were looking for proved to be very old indeed, and I've often wondered aloud at my luck for being 23 years old in a time and place in which only the past offers hope and inspiration; the future offers only artifice and blight. I travel now in a society of friends who heat their houses with hand-cut wood and eliminate in outhouses, who cut pine shingles with draw-knives and haul maple sugar sap on sleds, who weed potatoes with their university-trained hands, pushing long hair out of their way and thus marking their foreheads with beautiful penitent dust. We till the soil to atone for our fathers' destruction of it. We smell. We live far from the marketplaces in America by our own volition, and the powerful men left behind are happy to have us out of their way. They do not yet realize that their heirs will refuse to inhabit their hollow cities, will find them poisonous and lethal, will run back to the Stone Age if necessary for survival and peace.

Yet this canoe trip had to be made because there was adventure out there. We expected to find the Concord and Merrimack rivers polluted but still beautiful, and to witness firsthand the startling juxtaposition of old New England, land and water and mountains, and new America, factories and highways and dams; and to thus educate ourselves further in the works of God and man. We pushed on relentlessly, top speed 50 mph, in our eggshell Volkswagen (Hitler's manifestly correct conception of the common man's car), 100 miles to the sea. The week following, the week we'd spend in our canoe, was the very week when our countrymen would celebrate Columbus

Day (anniversary of the European discovery of Americans), the New York Mets in the World (American) Series, and the National Moratorium to demand an "early end to the war." Since we mourn the ruthless extinction of the natives, have outgrown baseball, and long ago commenced our own total Moratorium on constructive participation in this society, our presence and support was irrelevant to all of these national pastimes. We hoped only to paddle silently through the world, searching for traces of what has been lost.

Portsmouth was in an uproar.

* * *

George and Martha Dodge are the parents of the revolution as well as of seven sons, all of whom have now come home to Portsmouth, one of the oldest ports on the Atlantic side and of some importance to the United States Armed Forces. Gus, as he is nicknamed, is a respected physician in the city; Martha was a Nichols and still fries her own October donuts. Both are descendants of the oldest New England families, both old-fashioned, hospitable, warm, full of common sense, both admirers of Eldridge Cleaver and passionately involved, almost wracked, in attempts to right some of the American wrongs. In short, they are good candidates for an old homestead in Vermont, and yet themselves the most attractive natural resource left in Portsmouth. Another feature of the town is its extraordinary number (and quality) of 17th-century and 18th-century houses, built with virgin lumber which has yet to begin rotting or even chipping, but many of these houses are being stupidly and arbitrarily destroyed. (More about this in a moment.) Their sons, youngest first, are Peter, 14, who claims he can drive a motorcycle; Hovey, 16, who puts together electronic systems, including piecemeal stereo systems capable of blasting out "Goddamn the Pusher Man" and other hits from *Easy Rider* at astonishing volume and fidelity; Frank, 19, an accomplished cellist; Mark, 22, a soulful painter; Laurie, 25, a New Age carpenter; David, 27, a man of many pursuits who at the moment is restoring his house on South Street; and Buzzy, the oldest but no particular age, who can do anything.

It was Buzzy we had come to get, for Buzzy was our Native Indian Guide to the Concord and Merrimack rivers, and Buzzy could do anything. Had not Buzzy camped out at 60 below zero in Alaska? Wasn't it Buzzy who ran the rapids of the Pemigewasset? Didn't Buzzy fix the freezer with a clothespin or something? Buzzy can build a fire out of wet pine, sleep in a hollow log, make a shed into a mansion, or scale a snow-peaked mountain. If you are thinking of some perilous undertaking, my friend, my advice is to take Buzzy along. He is gifted with a calm and intelligent temperament, and a general all-around competence which is nothing less than astounding, particularly to half-freaked former militants trying gamely to live the life and discover what the planet is made up of. Mind you, Buzzy is no more remarkable than the rest of the Dodges, each in his or her fashion, but I haven't paper enough to go into the whole family (maybe some other time, over a fire, when we are alone), and the Dodges aren't seeking the publicity anyway. Buzzy and his wife, the former Erika Schmidt-Corvoisier, had been tripping around in Spain for a year or so there, but they were back in Portsmouth, now restoring from scratch an old house on Hanover Street and living in it with neither insulation in the walls nor a furnace in the basement, but with fireplaces older than anyone could remember. We apologized to Erika, Verandah and I, but we needed Buzzy for an historic river trip. She understood.

We went over to the main house, the Dodge Commune I called it, where the canoe was waiting for us, stored in the garage alongside children's bicycles, rakes, spare parts, nuts-and-bolts jar, the accumulation of seven sons' childhoods in Portsmouth by the sea. Our old friend Laurie, who lived with us in Vermont before the inexplicable magnet of Portsmouth drew him away, took us aside for a long walk through the Desolation Row of fine old buildings scheduled for demolition by Portsmouth Urban Renewal, and he showed us these houses from a carpenter's careful perspective. We touched the beams 14 inches thick, the planks wider than an arm-span, and gingerly stepped over broken glass where vandals had wrecked and robbed after the tenants of these buildings were forced to leave. There had been no protest over the demolition of the 17th-century in Portsmouth, not more than a whimper really, and I felt my long-dormant sense of outrage beginning to rekindle, and knew I had to split. For outrage leads to action, and action leads . . . where? Usually into a morass. It was strange, though, my outrage reborn not over some plan for future progressive society, but over concern for preservation of ancient hoary stuff from way back. That kind of stuff, I had always thought, is for Historical Society ladies. But when the whole world becomes one McDonald's Hamburger stand after another, you too will cry out for even a scrap of integrity.

Back at the Dodge Manse, everything was in healthy chaos as the entire family readied for a trip to Martha's mother's farm in Sturbridge, Mass. The driveway was lined with vehicles which showed the scars of their years of heavy use. Laurie's red pickup was chosen to carry the canoe, first to Sturbridge, then back to Boston (Cambridge), from which it would be driven on a friendly Volvo station wagon to Concord, Mass., where the river trip would begin. A lecturer from the University of New Hampshire appeared while Buzzy was going through the intense gymnastics required to fasten the canoe to the truck, and he stood by urging Buzz to come talk to his class about ecology and such while Buzzy said, "Yeah, sure" and "If I can find the time," all the while spinning Indian knots of every esoteric variety and the rest of the family carrying luggage (Hovey with his complete stereo system) for the two-day visit to the ancestral farm, and Dr. Gus looking angrily for the missing Peter. Laurie danced in his boots as he painted OCTOBER 15 in big black letters on the sides of the upturned canoe; good advertising for the Moratorium, he said, and even if the Moratorium showed signs of being a schmucky liberal thing, it was the best we had.

Porche and I hadn't counted on a Dodge excursion, and we found ourselves with two days to kill as Saturday dawned. To stay in Portsmouth with the Dodges all gone would have been too depressing, we agreed, so we repacked camping gear and artifacts of outdoor living into aforementioned VW, and decided to wait it out in old college hangouts, blast from the past, in Cambridge.

We split the map south along the green line designated as the Atlantic, uncomplicated by route numbers and little Esso markers, went to hole up in of all places, Cambridge.

Saturday: Danvers, Mass.

Interstate Route 95, like many another road in Massachusetts, is forever incomplete. The signs bravely contend that this Detour is merely Temporary, but the same Detour has existed since I was born and reared in these parts, and I cannot be convinced that Interstate Route 95 will ever be finished. For the time being, motorists (who probably deserve it) are required to get off 95—which is supposed to be a north-south road from Boston to Canada—at Topsfield, Mass., and take the last 15 miles into Boston on Route 1, assaulted on all sides by gas stations, boogie restaurants (Mr. Boogie, Boogie King, McDonald's Boogie, Boogie Delight, etc.), furniture outlets, pseudo-Native junk and tourist emporiums with names like Trading Post and Wampum Shop, drive-in movies; anything goes down on old Route 1.

21

In the course of effortlessly rolling south on the paved planet, however, we finally entered Danvers on old Route 1 and something in my head exploded. I had not been in Danvers for six or seven years, but it was the town where I had done four years once, as a student at St. John's Preparatory School, hereinafter called The Prep. I remembered that October was always spectacularly beautiful there, though I could recall little else good about The Prep. But here was I in Danvers once again and who knew how many years would pass before I'd be back? We pulled off the highway at the candy outlet and headed up Route 62, past the State Mental Hospital, where the old lady got on our bus every morning in 1960 and asked us "Is your name John? Is it Peter?"

I have had some experience with mental hospitals in Massachusetts, though never, through chance or whatever, as an inmate; but I could never tell you in mere words the horror and despair they enclose in vain striving to rid the air in the Commonwealth of beserk and helpless vibrations. The Commonwealth as a whole is full of nightmares, universities, and museums aside or perhaps inclusive; all the authorities out of control, people getting screwed right and left, but whaddya gonna do kid all the politishun's crooked everybody knows.

I have also had some experience with Roman Catholicism, which is still alive in Massachusetts, where it too is out of control. They say there is no more virulent anti-Catholic than a former one; I'm living proof of the bigotry that comes of rebellion to indoctrination. Recent news reports, which one can never trust, indicate that it is slowly dying of its own anachronisms but I have seen too many millions of crucifix-kissing 8-year-olds to be satisfied with gradual progress. Listen, the Stephen Daedalus withdrawal, which began for me at puberty, ain't no joke, and it is thoroughly avoidable.

"What kind of a school is this?" Verandah asked as we pulled uphill to the lofty and expensive spires of The Prep, where some kind of Parents' Weekend was evidently in progress. Well, it's a school which houses the dead. The dead me resides there still. It's a school where terror of God is a tool, where violence between teacher and student was common, where sex was reserved for toilet stalls. This school was nowhere to go on a fine Saturday afternoon, yet there we were and all the parents looking shocked and the dolled-up Brothers looking confused.

Once a Catlick, always a Catlick, that's what really scared me I suppose. These guys and the Good Sisters before them really did a job on me, and I feared getting out of the friendly VW would expose me to the germs of the old disease, that I'd meet some former teacher who'd ask me had I been keeping the faith, and I'd mumble something indistinct because I couldn't summon the audacity to rant and scream, "You mothers are going to pay for all this!" as would have been appropriate. Actually they might never have asked me about the faith for my opinions are well-understood at The Prep, or so an old school friend, now a Marine lieutenant in Vietnam, once told me; he said I had the status of a What-Went-Wrong case there. But we did get out of the car and we walked around the neatly mowed grass and under the glowing October trees now dull in comparison to Vermont and overshadowed, as they were landscaped to be, by the crosses and towers of the old school. I didn't meet any old teachers and I never introduced myself to anybody. I did try to talk to one old friend but the secretary informed me that some of the Brothers had gone out with some of the Boys and my friend was not around. Out with the Boys, all of whom we encountered looked strictly 1955, short hair and ties, and I knew the poor bastards would mostly all miss the boat, just as most of my classmates did. Missing the boat is just about the worst thing can happen to a young man in America today, for where is he if he's still on the other side? In the company of the constipated, that's where. The best way he can phrase his situation is in terms of reform—he is reforming the churches, schools, corporations, by belonging to them. "Well, that's fine if it's the best you can do," say the self-righteous freaks from their tight-knit brotherhood of hair and leisure and though my opinions belong to the latter class, my heart goes out to the lonely ones who missed that goddamn boat and will never see another chance.

We all got on the boat late in life, I understand, and perhaps our children if we can overcome our fear of bringing them into the world, perhaps they will be afloat from the first. That sort of apparent progress would be gratifying, and I have met wonderful Acid Children in my time. This interlude is over. We raced back to the car and resumed our path to Cambridge, watching the signs carefully to avoid the big big hex in this, the traditional Season of the Witch in New England.

Sunday: Cambridge, Mass.

I was reading the Boston Sunday Globe Financial Section for lack of other employment or reading matter when I came upon a news account of the spectacular success of a chain of artsie-fartsie shops called Cambridge Spice and Tea Exporters (or something close to that). These shops sell ornaments for the home, bamboo ding-dongs to hang over the window, incense, colorful but useless items of all sorts; and the proprietor was there quoted to the effect that the word "Cambridge" on the shops gives them a magic quality that brings in the bread right quick. And of course! Funny I never realized it before, but Cambridge is the home base, one of the centers, at least, of useless conceits for the affluent American, including the longhaired variety. Harvard University, if I may say so, could vanish tomorrow (in fact it *may*) with no appreciable loss to the physical or intellectual health of the nation. Those who wished to study Catullus would continue to do so; and those whose lives are considerably less earnest would doubtless find some other occupation, perhaps more rewarding, than hanging out in the Yard. The great irony of Cambridge is that, despite its vaunted status as a center of the arts, education, technology, and political wisdom, it is in reality a Bore. It stultifies, rather than encourages, productive thought and employment, by throwing up countless insuperable obstacles to peace of mind and simple locomotion from one place to another. Why, if all the creative energy expended in Cambridge on paying telephone bills, signing documents, finding a cab, buying a milkshake, bitching at the landlord and shoplifting from the Harvard Coop could be channeled into writing, playing, loving, and working, the results would probably be stupendous. At the moment, it is simply a marketplace of fatuous ideas and implements for those who seek to amuse themselves while Babylon falls around them. Thoreau on Boston:

> I see a great many barrels and fig-drums—piles of wood for umbrella-sticks,—blocks of granite and ice,—great heaps of goods, and the means of packing and conveying them,—much wrapping-paper and twine,—many crates and hogsheads and trucks,—and that is Boston. The more barrels, the more Boston. The museums and scientific societies and libraries are accidental. They gather around the sands to save carting. The wharf-rats and customhouse officers, and broken-down poets, seeking a fortune amid the barrels. (*Cape Cod*)

There are some useful items to be purchased in Cambridge (and Boston) but they are hard to find; it is next to impossible, for example, to find oak beams for building, spare uncut wood for burning, or fresh vegetables for eating, and certainly not worth the trouble you would encounter in getting them—unless you are inextricably bound to the city. Similarly, there are many men and women worth meeting there, people whose lives are neither devoted to poisoning the environment and water nor to idle and dispassionate amusements, but I have found such folks increasingly difficult to locate. You remember so-and-so who used to live on Brookline Street? Split to the Coast. Somebody else is in Nova Scotia, many are in Vermont, a few have taken to caves in Crete, a whole group went way up in British Columbia. Perhaps I am speaking only of a limited generational attitude, surely the managers of Cambridge corporations and deans of the schools have not all split too, but I know there is more to it than youth and mobility, more than that youthful restlessness which George Apley was sent to Europe to work off. No, there's a definite panic on the hip scene in Cambridge, people going to uncommonly arduous lengths (debt, sacrifice, the prospect of cold toes and brown rice forever) to get away while there's still time. Although we grew up, intellectually and emotionally at least, in Cambridge, and once made the big scene there in scores of apartments and houses, V and I now could find only one friendly place to lay our heads and weary bums, and that was at Peter Simon's. We went looking for Peter's head of wild curly red hair, he looks like a freaked-out Howdy Doody really, a photographer, sure that when we found it there'd be new Beatles and Band music, orange juice in the frig, place to take your shoes off; and so there was.

We had brought along for the canoe trip the kinds of things that made sense: sleeping bags, tarp, tools, cooking utensils, potatoes and other vegetables we'd grown in the summer, several gallons of honest-to-God Vermont water (no bacterial content) in the event the waters of the Merrimack should be beyond boiling. We couldn't bake bread on the river banks, surely, as we do at home, and, sensing that Henry's advice on buying bread from farmers just didn't apply these days, I went to a local sooper-dooper and acquired two loaves of Yah-Yah Bread at 20 cents the loaf and, almost as an afterthought, got a jar of Skippy Peanut Butter for about 40 cents. The Yah-Yah Bread was packed in a psychedoolic magenta plastic with cartoons of hipsters (one boy, one girl) on the outside and Avalon Ballroom lettering, the kind you must twist your head to read, so it did catch my eye. And I have liked Skippy since I discovered (1) peanuts will not grow very well in Vermont, (2) the jar can be used as a measuring cup (but only when it's empty), (3) the Skippy heiress is 22 and some kind of pill freak who busts up cocktail parties in New York. I noticed that the Skippy contained no BHA or BHT but that the Yah-Yah Bread did; these chemicals are often called "preservatives," and although I can't responsibly suggest they will kill *you*, they do contain the element which makes most commercial foods taste *dead*. We have found that an astonishingly wide variety of food items contain BHA or BHT or both, so I can only conclude that most of my countrymen subsist on the stuff. They are hooked. The sole advantage of preservatives to the consumer, it seems, is that he can now save money by buying day-old or month-old baked goods and be certain that they will taste like cold putty no matter their birthday. We did spend a goodly part of the harvest season giving away all the fruits and vegetables we couldn't use to city people (old friends and family) who freaked on what a tomato, or a peach, really is. The middle-aged and elderly ones remembered; the young ones learned. One and all reflected on how sinister and subtle the Dead Food craze came on, how you didn't notice it taking over until it was too late. The old Victory Garden thing may be in for a revival, friends, but I suspect it will reach only a marginal part of the population, the others will be too busy at the shop or office, dump DDT or other chemical killers on their crop, or be afraid to eat an ear of corn that's white, a tomato with a hole in it, a carrot with dirt on it. Tough luck for them what think it's Easier to go to the sooper-dooper and get those nice *clean* apples wrapped in cellophane, uniform in size and shining like mirrors, the kind I have never seen growing on any tree. How about *you?*

We escaped the supermarket, thus, without being tempted by the Meat, Poultry, or Vegetable departments, not to mention the paperbacks and plants. And we then did what everybody does in Cambridge, which amounted to what Bob Dylan called Too Much of Nothing. We waited for the morning to come, the daybreak which would put us on the rivers in our canoe at last; we got stoned and listened to the Beatles; we got bored and went out to spend some money, finally choosing a hip movie-house on Massachusetts Avenue and killing some hours with old Orson Welles. We did not get raped, mugged, or robbed as it turned out. We heard the noises and smelled the smells, drank the water and breathed the air. It was altogether quite a risky adventure. Our guides, Plucky Peter and his lady-friend Nancy, who is *only 17,* could not have been more hospitable and reassuring; in fact, they agreed to accompany us on parts of the river trip, grateful for some excuse to cut boring college classes they said. And Nancy even cooked a fine meal out of some farm vegetables on a stove which produced instant heat from gasoline which comes from under the street!

The canoe arrived after dark, good old Buzzy with it spinning yarns of rapids and dams, islands to camp on (the name Merrimack meant to the natives "river of many islands"), wild animules, the likelihood of rain. He and Verandah went to sleep early, I stayed up nervously watching commercials on television (including one post-midnight Stoned Voice urging kids not to smoke dope *because it's illegal*), went to sleep on the floor and dreamed of wild muskrats and other creatures of the past.

Monday: Concord, Mass.

Monday dawned quietly even in the Hub of the Universe for Monday this time around was a Holiday, the day after Columbus Day. I guessed that those who had gone off on three-day weekends had not yet returned, and the others were all sleeping late; because here it was Monday morning, and Central Square was not putrid with humanity, just a few winos hanging around and no policemen for traffic. The canoe advertising OCTOBER 15 was loaded onto Peter's Volvo while I hurry-hid my VW in the neighbor Harry's backyard; Harry was not around anyway, Harry had split to Vermont, but I left Harry a note explaining that since his backyard was full of garbage anyway, it might as well have my VW. Our canoe was 18 feet long and three feet wide, bright orange, and aluminum. Buzzy had fashioned wheels for it out of a block of wood and two old tricycle wheels, not unlike Thoreau's contraption I thought; they gave the canoe a faithful if bumpy ride around dams and such.

We took Route 2 past the shopping plazas and biochemical warfare factories out to Concord. There are two sets of signs in Concord, one leading to Walden, the other to the Concord Reformatory. The former is a state park with rules and regulations posted on the trees, the latter a prison for boys with a fancy-pants highway sign in front: "Welcome to Concord, Home of Emerson, Thoreau and the Alcotts." The Reformatory, a vast grey dungeon, is complemented by a farm where, I am told, the Boys learn vital agricultural skills. And not a few other tricks. The Brothers and the Boys. Pity the Boy who grows up in Massachusetts, if she has as many greystone towers to enclose him as it seems.

We stopped for advice, which way to the Concord River please, at a gas station. The man there obliged us, but all the while acting like we were wasting his valuable time. There were no other customers. The spot he led us to proved to be a park, full of monuments and walkways, grass mowed as with a Gillette Techmatic but a lovely spot notwithstanding. As we readied the canoe for embarkment, a uniformed gent approached us grimly, and I was sure there'd be some Commonwealth law against canoes but no, he merely wanted to admire the rig and satisfy his curiosity. It is quite legal to launch your boat in Concord still, though they have placed speed limit signs on the bridges ("River Speed Limit: 10 MPH ENFORCED."), and so we rolled ours to what looked like a good place and waited a moment, very like the moment you take before diving off a high covered bridge into a gurgling fresh-water pond in July. Peter took funny-face pictures while a small band of strollers, tourists, or townspeople who can tell the difference, leaf-peepers we called them because they took Kodak Brownie shots of this or that red tree, gathered about to watch and wave. There was no obvious animosity between us this bright morning, for unlike the gas station, the place itself was beautiful, we were together, and it was a great day for a boat trip. Something in all men smiles on the idea of a cruise up the planet. We knew we'd be heading downstream, or north, to the mouth of the Merrimack, but the river itself had no easily discernible current; rather it looked from the shore like a quiet and friendly scar on the earth, made of such stuff you could put your foot through. Buzzy knew by some mysterious instinct which way was north, but I argued the point for a while. Then, as we were climbing into our silent craft, a noisy crowd of Canadian honkers drifted into view overhead, flying

V-formation (V for victory, Vietnam, Verandah, Vermont) due south, and I declare even the tired holiday crowd broke into smiles. Canadian geese over Concord, it's enough to make you believe in God.

> The Musketaquid, or Grass-ground River, though probably as old as the Nile or Euphrates, did not begin to have a place in civilized history until the fame of its grassy meadows and its fish attracted settlers out of England in 1635, when it received the other but kindred name of CONCORD from the first plantation on its banks, which appears to have been commenced in a spirit of peace and harmony. It will be Grass-ground River as long as grass grows and water runs here; it will be Concord River only while men lead peaceable lives on its banks. To an extinct race it was grass-ground, where they hunted and fished; and it is still perennial grass-ground to Concord farmers, who own the Great Meadows, and get the hay from year to year.

Of course, get the hay! But the Great Meadows are mostly woods now, called the Great Meadows National Wildlife Refuge according to the brightly painted signs posted here and there on the banks, obviously intended for the information of those who would ride the river in boats. And as we paddled along, we did meet other boats, speedboats mostly with vroom-vroom motors and gaseous fumes who circled our canoe and laughed as it rocked in the unnatural waves of their passing. And one old couple, strictly Monet, paddling a tiny wisp of a canoe. Despite everything, though, the land *did* goddamn it open in a great vista, rising up on both sides to support scampering squirrels and the like, and while it lasted, the National Wildlife Refuge seemed to me a worthy piece of territory.

Buzzy tired of the paddles before Porche and I did, and over our protests, elected to turn on his pint-sized outboard, which went bap-bap rather than vroom-vroom, and moved the canoe no faster than the paddles but with less effort on our part, of course. I used this respite from work to survey the terrain with the close eye of loving ignorance, and I watched the Wildlife Refuge become plain old Concord and a pastel ranch house come into view. Everything moved so slowly, it was like a super-down drug, and we were spared no details of this modern American prefab architecture—and, beyond it, the rising towers of yon civilization. Fishermen began to appear, at first alone and then in groups; and though we dutifully inquired of each what he had caught that morning, we never found a man with so much as a catfish to show for his efforts. Clearly, I thought, it is Columbus Day (or the day after) and these people are fishing for old times' sake and not in hopes of actually catching something. The last group of fishers were segregated—a half-dozen white people on one side of the Concord, and as many black people on the other. The river was narrow and shallow enough at that point to walk across, so I guessed that these people wanted it that way, preferred at least to do their fruitless casting among friends. Soon enough, several hours later, we were in Carlisle, at the Carlisle Bridge, and I'd become concerned that the river still showed no sign of a current. It was just about standing still and we the only moving things in the landscape. Verandah trailed her fingers through the water from the bow. From my perch in the center, I remarked, "It's pretty but it's dead."

"Maybe we're dead" was all she said.

*   *   *

From Carlisle, where we met Peter Simon and enjoyed a Skippy and Yah-Yah lunch, we went on to Billerica with high hopes of making Lowell that day and thus getting over the New Hampshire border the next. For reasons obviously unassociated with fact, I expected the scenery, colors, and water in New Hampshire to be superior to those in Massachusetts, and we reassured ourselves that, bad as the Concord was now becoming, we were at least taking the worst medicine first. The entrance to Billerica by water resembles the old MGM views of distant forts in the wild West; for the first sign of the approaching town is an American flag flapping in the breeze like somebody's long-johns on the line, and planted on top of a hideous redbrick mill with a mammoth black smokestack. No smoke today, though, for it was a holiday remember (and we do need constant reminders on days like Columbus Day and Washington's Birthday, so difficult has it become for us to *relate* to them), and the only sign of life was a wilted elderly watchman, who sat behind the factory gates merely watching cars go by. The mill, called North Billerica Company (presumably manufacturers of North Billericas), was built on a dam which we didn't notice until we very nearly went over it, and seemed to be rooted in the water itself. That is, the sides of the buildings extended below the riverline, making the banks absolutely inaccessible except through the mill-yard itself, for several hundred yards. And the watchman, clearly, was the old Keeper of the Locks whom Henry had charmed into letting him pass on the Sabbath. Thus did this kind man unchain the gates of the North Billerica Company and lead us through to the safe side of the dam—where, for the first time, we paddled through water actually being used, before our very eyes, as an open sewer. Worse yet, we recognized that the scuz and sludge pouring forth from the mill through 6-inch drainpipes would follow us downstream, that it was in fact better to navigate on dead but quiet waters than on water teeming with Elimination, at times even belching out gaseous bubbles, and smelling like fresh bait for tsetse flies and vultures. From North Billerica to the end of our journey, we would see only two other craft on these waters, one a crude raft bearing three boys (more or less 10-years-old) and a smiling dog, straight Huck Finn stuff but the kids said not a word as we passed them by, and the other a hardware-store rubber bathtub floating two

13- or 14-year-old boys who were headed for Concord Reformatory, you could just tell. This latter pair were reincarnations of the Bad Boys I'd known back in Lawrence, which is on the Merrimack, boys whom I had joined in some Bad adventures on the river until I finally couldn't make their grade.

Boys will find charm in junk, as every red-blooded smalltown scoutmaster knows; boys will hang around burned-out houses, old railroad yards, town dumps, the backs of breweries, and find there unlimited access to toys for the body and mind. We met these two as our canoe bumped to a stop against huge rocks surrounding a factory which had burned to the ground, only the smokestack erect, nobody else around, as we hauled our gear out of the boat onto broken glass and pieces of brick and charred timbers that fell through when you stepped on them, in this unspeakably North Vietnamese place, Dresden in Billerica, this corner of Massachusetts which could be the scene after World War III. The boys informed us in a heavy local accent—Oh yah, Oh yah—that we'd pass "three rapids and a dam" before the Concord emptied into the Merrimack in Lowell, then left us alone again. Buzzy ran the first set of rapids alone while Verandah and I hauled knapsacks and sleeping bags, paddles and outboard, through the wreckage to the place where the river deepened. It was then that we began to notice the trees, even the trees in this place were palsied and skinny, their colors muted. An old stump I was using for support caved in on me. And to venture anywhere near the trees or brush meant to be covered with clinging brown dead burrs, pickies I call them, that fall into your socks and irritate your skin. We were grateful to get back in the canoe and leave that nightmare once-and-past factory behind. It was the worst place I had ever lived, a place where nothing could be salvaged, not even a piece of wire or useful stick on the ground.

A mile or so downstream, just south of Lowell we reckoned, the second set of rapids began and the canoe quickly became trapped between and on top of rocks which shared the water now with old tires, a refrigerator, a washing machine, wrecked cars and trucks, metal hoops, and bobbing clumps of feces. Verandah had to get out in midstream to lighten our load, and she disappeared into the pickies. A little later, I too got out as the canoe turned sideways, broadstream, and Buzzy warned in a calm and dejected tone, "We are going to capsize very soon, we will capsize if we don't get out of here." Boots tied about my neck and dungarees rolled up over my knees, there's me slipping on rocks slimy with who wants to know what, making for a bank which appears impossible to scale. I lost sight of Buzzy as the canoe bounced and careened downstream, but caught Verandah in my free eye, silently waiting for me at the top of the rise. The current, which was imperceptible before, was ferocious now, as the shallow water rushed downhill over rocks left there by the Billerica dams; and more than once I felt myself falling over them, too, breaking bones I thought in my mad rush to the sea on a road greased with shit. The bank, when I reached it, was knee-deep in garbage of all kinds—metal, paper, and glass. Rolls of toilet paper had been strung like Christmas tinsel on the brittle limbs of the trees, and cardboard containers by the hundreds, flattened by snow and made soggy by rain, had formed layers of mush. I was the creature from the black lagoon, or a soul in purgatory, stretching forth his hand for a lift out of my slime from the mysterious beautiful lady Up There.

When the ascent was made and breaths caught, we discovered ourselves in a railroad yard whose tracks were varnished amber with rust and freight cars left there, open, to suffer all weather and never move again. Union Pacific, they proudly announced. Nobody was around. I fancied myself a television reporter for some new galaxy, bringing the folks back home a documentary of the continent on Earth that died; "it all began to break down, folks, in fourteen hundred and ninety-two, when Columbus sailed the ocean blue. To an extinct race, it was grass-ground river."

We walked the graveled planet now for maybe a half-mile, shouting for Buzzy from time to time. We found him at the end of the third set of rapids with gloom all over his face. The canoe took a bad leap, he said, the outboard was lost somewhere under water too black to reveal it, the Yah-Yah bread soaked to the consistency of liquid BHT, all the bedding and clothing and food dripping wet.

And the sun was setting somewhere but we could not see it.

And the air was turning colder though we couldn't say why.

And the land was impossible to camp on, it would be a bed of broken glass and rusty nails.

Clearly we could only push on to Lowell, where Peter Simon had been waiting hours for us no doubt, and push we did until we floated into the heart of that town after dark, almost bumping the edge of a vast dam in our blindness, then groping and paddling back and forth across this Concord to find a bank which was neither solid vertical concrete nor sealed off by a high chain-link fence, operating by the light of *The Lowell Sun* neon billboard and finally hauling OCTOBER 15 from the water behind a taxicab garage and wheeling it through the crowded center of town, wondering where we could safely be alive.

Lowell is a sister-city to Lawrence and Haverhill, all three being one-river towns born of the "industrial revolution" and very close in spirit to those almost-charming images of factory-towns in British literature from Blake to the Beatles. Ethnic neighborhoods remain and national churches (mostly Catholic) thrive there still—the Greeks still fiercely chauvinistic, the French Canadians still hard drinkers, the Italians still fond of block parties in honor of the Three Saints. There is a strikingly 19th-century downtown area but, despite the energetic promotion of the oldest merchants in town, it is slowly corroding as it loses ground to the highway shopping plazas. Life there is sooty, and even the young people look hard and wrinkled. Though it is only a stone's throw from cultured, boring Boston, it may as well be a thousand miles away for all the intellectual influence it has absorbed. We didn't know it at the moment we were strolling down Central Street with the canoe between us, but Peter Simon had earlier fled the city, terrified at the fierce looks and obscene catcalls which his long hair had provoked. I was not afraid, though, for I knew that the natives, while resenting our freedom, were yet too pacified and dulled by their daily lives to risk energetic hostility on us. Strangers may securely enough walk the streets of Lowell, Lawrence, or Haverhill, for the locals will kill only each other. Arriving in Lowell was for me a grand homecoming.

Kerouac came back to Lowell after all those years making scenes, and that has scared me crazy since I've known who Kerouac was. "If all else fails," I thought, "we could always go see Kerouac, maybe he'd put us up." Came back to Lowell even though nobody goes anywhere from there, he must have come back to die, that's the only thing makes sense by the gee. Stopped writing he did, just sat there in crummy Lowell with beer and television, and *The Lowell Sun* at four in the afternoon, delivered by the local altar boy at Saint Ann's, or Sacred Heart, or Saint Pat's. Was he an altar boy, choir boy, chief Boy Scout, candidate for the priesthood, did he win a Ladies Sodality scholarship to The Prep? God, Kerouac, did you have a paper route too and hit all the bars on Christmas Eve? Christ, Kerouac, you're blowing my mind living in Lowell, will you never go back to Big Sur? Kerouac, listen: Frost came from Lawrence, too, hey from my neighborhood in South Lawrence, but he *got out* man and he didn't come back. Robert Frost! And didn't Jack Kennedy make him poet laureate or something? Kerouac, see: Leonard *Bernstein* came from here, but *he* got out! Everybody from Lowell and Lawrence had half a break in this world *split*. You stay here, you're as good as dead baby.

I wanted to go get Kerouac and put him in the middle of the canoe with his bottle and take him north to New Hampshire. Instead, I went looking for my younger brother Rick but his Greek landlord said he moved to a street that don't *exist* any more in Lowell. "Your brother hiza nice boy, I tell him 'two things, Rick: don't smoke no marihoony, geta you degree!' " I used to think a degree was the only ticket out of Lawrence and Lowell, too, but here I am on Central Street with my canoe!

We were befriended by a corpulent Boston *Record-American* reporter (Hearst sheet, cheesecake and crime mostly), who put us and the canoe on the back of his truck which he normally uses for carting secondhand furniture; man's got to make a living. He was also, he said, a member of the Lowell police force and found out about us from the police radio's moment-by-moment broadcast report of our progress through the city. He called the cops on a street-side phone and arranged for us to sleep on the Boulevard river bank, past all the dams and fetid canals of Lowell, and there we took our rest at last. The Boulevard traffic passed several yards from our heads at 60 and 70 miles per hour, and some local teenagers drove their jalopy up to our encampment with bright lights on at 2 or 3 A.M. The bank was littered with broken beer bottles, but I slept soundly nonetheless. We had no food now, so I got up in the night and walked up the Boulevard to where I knew an all-night pizza stand existed; and, in the process, bumped into a parked car with two kids fucking noisily in the back seat. Of course, I thought, Lowell is the last place on the planet where kids still ball in dad's car because there is no place to go, there are no private apartments for kids or independent kid-societies. Walking back with coffee-cake and hamburgers, I noticed dozens of parked cars just off the road, a road without sidewalks, where nobody but me had walked for a long time. And just before I got back to our encampment, I met an old man with whiskey on his breath who looked me straight in the eye and said, "Going to Lawrence?"

Around midnight, a group of married couples arrived with Dunkin Donuts for us to eat; they had heard of the legendary canoe, it was all over town, they wanted to see if it was really so. One man used to fish for salmon in the Merrimack, but he "wouldn't piss in it now." His wife blamed the rich people who own the mills, they are the ones she said who have destroyed the water. All who came to talk with us that night said how many years had passed since they last saw a real boat seriously navigating up the Merrimack River. "Are you sure," one woman asked in a harsh voice, "nobody's makin ya do it?"

Tuesday: Lowell, Mass.

Culture-hero Steve McQueen has said, "I would rather wake up in the middle of nowhere than in any city on Earth." Naturally, I second that. Morning in Lowell cannot properly be called "sunrise," for it is the General Electric plant and not the burning star which first appears on the horizon. Our *Record-American* reporter friend returned to take pictures of us for his newspaper but we waited around a long time hoping for Peter Simon to arrive in the magic Volvo which could both fetch new groceries and go searching for the lost outboard. We would be paddling upstream now, and in the face of a stiff wind, so the motor might have proved useful in a pinch. But there was no Peter, no coffee, no breakfast and no hope, so we shoved off at 9 A.M., with only the Boston *Record-American* for witness. We had camped, it turned out, next to a row of garbage cans on which somebody in Lowell (maybe someday she'll come come come along) had painted peace signs and slogans like "Smile on your brother" and "Let's clean up Big Muddy." It was a noble but pathetic gesture, this youthful assumption that the Dirt in the Merrimack was nothing worse than Mud, and that it could be cleaned up if only each of us smiled more. As the rows of factories proved beyond doubt, and there is something hard and undeniable in this, Lowell would cease to be Lowell if it did not pollute the Merrimack River. Lowell and its sister-cities create shoes, textiles, and paper for you and me—who, as literate people, do not live on the Merrimack River anyway. The industries in Lowell pay their employees very poorly indeed, yet their profits cannot be what they used to be, for the shops are slowly and one-by-one closing down. We paddled furiously against the wind to get the hell out, aiming ourselves toward Tyngsboro by noon and Nashua, New Hampshire, by nightfall.

The Merrimack is substantially wider and deeper than the Concord, a real river and not just a stream, so for the first time I felt that flush of anxiety which comes after knowing you are too far-out to swim back in the event of trouble. It was back-aching work but we could manage about two miles per hour, which seemed to me fast enough for any sensible voyage. I set myself little targets, such as the big drive-in movie screen on Route 113, and overtook each one in my stride. I enjoy slow progress and gradual change in my own life as much as I deplore it in social trends; but I am sufficiently tuned-in to the century to realize that we men never really get *anywhere*. It's always more of the same, so to speak—birth, life, death, walking abroad in a shower of your days, how soon having Time the subtle thief of youth stealing on his wing your three-and-twentieth year, etc. etc. Life does move exquisitely slow, all the crap in newspapers about "revolutionary developments" aside, and we do tend to end up where we started. The absurdity of our situation, too, lay in the fact that we could have gotten from Lowell to Tyngsboro in three minutes rather than three hours, but there was no reason to go to

Tyngsboro *anyway* as none of us believed it would be the idyllic spot Henry described; thus we never felt we were *wasting time*.

Two or three miles up from Lowell, as we paddled through water absolutely white with swirling pools of some awful chemical substance, we heard Peter Simon's voice calling as from afar. He and Nancy were on the opposite bank, trapped in the Volvo by a pack of ravenous house-dogs, yet overjoyed to have found us again. We paddled over to them and mutually decided on a spot just up a piece to disembark and confer. Verandah and Nancy stayed behind to cook a breakfast of oatmeal and eggs while we menfolk took off in the car to look for that outboard, got a flat on the Boulevard, got soaking wet, got in trouble with an elderly French Canadian lady who objected to Buzzy's using her backyard as an approach to the river until I calmed her in the best Lawrence-Lowell half-Canuck accent I could muster from memories of my grandmother. In all, got nothing accomplished and returned to the breakfast site close to noon, Peter swearing it was gonna rain and Buzzy just swearing. The outboard had cost B his last 60 dollars, and was purchased especially for this trip; moreover, he was beginning to feel sick in the stomach, and wondered just what poisons we might be picking up from the fair Merrimack.

I wanted Pierre to join us at that point, abandon his car and get on the boat. Fancying myself Kesey and all of us Merry Pranksters, I said, "Peter, you must be On the Boat or Off the Boat." But Tuesday was a Mets day, Peter said, and though he would follow us upstream and generally watch out, he must stay close to the car radio to keep tabs on Tom Seaver and so-and-so's stealing third. It meant nothing to me, but since Peter thought it was important, who was I to belittle it? Some people get their energy off Kesey and Kerouac and Thoreau, others off Seaver and Swoboda; stocks and bonds, movies and periodicals, movements and rallies, rivers and oceans, balls and strikes; you name it, somebody lives on it. Friends of mine have been addicted to such dangerous drugs as television, bourbon, and The New York Times, daily *and* Sunday. I myself have been addicted to Pall Mall Cigarettes for years, and have more than once gone hungry to support my habit; I am also a Black Coffee freak, and have been known to drink 15 to 20 cups in a day. Everything in me which responds to reason prays for the imminent day when mass-produced and commercially distributed goods will simply stop coming, all the bright red Pall Mall trucks will break down in North Carolina and all the Colombian coffee boats rot in their harbors. Then we, poor weaklings, will have at least a chance to aspire to that personal independence which we all so desperately need. We will be addicted to making do for ourselves, each of us will be President of the United States and responsible for the social welfare of the whole world, we will rise to our godheads at the same time we stoop to gather scrap wood for the fire. We will be able to afford, then, to offer and accept a little help from our friends.

So Peter was hooked on the Mets and there seemed no solution but to plan the rest of the trip *around* this handicap. Peter had to break camp early, drive to towns for newspaper reports of the previous day's game, leave the canoe to its own progress while he sought out television stores where the American Series would be coming across display color sets, return to us radiant with news of the latest victories. The Mets were *winners* at least, that's more than I could say for Pall Malls—which I consumed, though moderately, throughout the journey.

These pathetic addictions came together in Tyngsboro in an odd fashion. When we arrived at the bridge there, Peter was nowhere to be found, off watching the Mets; and we three were out of cigarettes and of course carrying no money. Buzzy, to the rescue, found a selection of old two-cent and nickel soda pop bottles imbedded in the silt bank, and cashed them in for a pack of smokes at the variety store conveniently located on top of the bank. All else we found there was a single half-rotted sunfish, five inches or so, washed ashore.

We were always looking for "a nice little island" on which to camp. The only one we found that day was King's Island, which is now a golf course with buildings, garages, a bar, and a bridge to the highway. Three lady golfers, the kind with jewel-encrusted sunglasses roped to their necks on aluminum chains, spied us from the ninth hole, and one chirped, "Well isn't that *adorable*." A painted sign on the bank read "Watch out for golf balls," and the river around the island had obviously become a God-made water trap for the wives of the Lowell-Nashua managerial class. It became evident near here, too, that many of the houses along the banks had eliminated the need for septic tanks by flushing directly into the river through underground pipes.

Both Buzzy and Verandah being now sick at their centers, and the prospect of sleeping in industrial Nashua too bleak to consider, we elected after much procrastination to drive around that city altogether, and thus ended up resuming the trip and camping out in Bow Junction, New Hampshire, birthplace of Mary Baker Eddy. Peter parked the Volvo on what we assumed to be a lonely access road and we paddled to what looked like a stretch of serious forest, arriving there just in time to spread out a few tarps and start a fire before dark fell. Stumbling about in the night in search of a place to Eliminate, I discovered that the woods were only 30 to 40 feet wide, bordered by the river on one side and a real, if dirt, road on the other; and they were only a quarter-mile long, bordered by immense machines of one kind or other on either end. The access road was studded with houses suburban-style, whose lights shined brightly at us and were reflected in the water, and the traffic on it sounded high-speed. We had been once more cruelly tricked. Sirens filled the air and our heads. Brakes screeched and a metallic thud bounced off our ears. The quiet but persistent rumble of technology charged the atmosphere, never letting up; it was the trembling of the earth which you, friend, can hear tonight if you but focus your attention on it. The earth is crying, what can I do to help it? Give it a Demerol?

Wednesday: Bow Junction, N.H.

I love man-kind but I hate the institutions of the dead unkind. Men execute nothing so faithfully as the wills of the dead, to the last codicil and letter. *They* rule this world, and the living are but their executors.
　　　　　　　　　　　　　　　　　　　　　—Thoreau,
A Week on the Concord and Merrimack Rivers

When we were babes in college and thought ourselves the only people in America smart enough to be unilaterally opposed to the United States' presence in Vietnam, we'd sit around the Protestant house at B.U., though we were none of us Protestants, and say, "This war won't end until every mother who loses a son, every wife who loses a husband, knows that their men died *in vain*." As long as the families of the 42,000 dead in fruitless combat could congratulate themselves on giving a boy to a good cause, more deaths would be unavoidable, we analyzed. It seemed the very will of the dead that America continue its genocidal assault on the East, the voices of those Southside Bad Boys crying out "Get him back, Emile!" to the runty kid from Sacre Coeur Parish. I'm not sure when this attitude began to corrode, sometimes I flatter myself with the thought that I did my part to bring it about (though a fat lot of good it has done over *there*); but I see with my own eyes that the wife of a dead Marine in Manchester, New Hampshire, on the Merrimack, refuses to have her husband's coffin draped in the Stars and Stripes. There is great mourning in New Hampshire over a group of six men who come back in boxes; five are buried with all attendant military honors, the sixth with Bob Dylan and angry rhetoric. In Manchester, New Hampshire, the most reactionary town in all of New England. So the will of the dead *now* is that we take revenge on the government, on Lyndon Johnson (remember that stinker?) and Richard Nixon and Lew Hershey, McNamara, Rusk, Rostow, Clifford, Laird, Westmoreland, Abrams, as if these men together and alone caused it to happen, and not the entire lot of us. The American people, in taking revenge on the gooks, have all but destroyed the paradisial terrain and refined culture of Vietnam; now they will turn on themselves and do the same at home. What is ambiguously called "the system" will crumble and fall, it is all too clear. The economy, military effectiveness, control and discipline of the young, none of these is looking too good for "the system." What will replace it? Does it matter?

After Marshall Bloom's suicide, I was exhorted by some old friends to come back to Washington, where my personal adventure with Bloom began, and rip up a cloud in the streets; have a reunion with my former allies in the movement. I declined. Just as I have avoided Chicago, Berkeley, New York City, even Woodstock, where all the heavy scenes have been going down, I shall absent myself from Washington on November 15. For I am choosing to refuse to execute the wills of the dead. Marshall had asked me, in his note, to be an executor of sorts, distributing his personal things from a second-floor closet at the farm to his friends around the country and on the farms; but I can't even do that, at least I haven't been able to yet.

The New York Times seized on Marshall's death to print a five-column headline, "Suicide Puzzles Friends of Founder of Radical News Service," and an article which mocked his conviction that activists will move to rural areas because "the city burns people out." *The Times* suggested that the last laugh was on Marshall and his friends, for while the citified branch of our Liberation News Service was still churning out propaganda from Claremont Avenue in New York, we were running vacuum-cleaner hoses from exhaust pipes into vent windows and expiring of despair. And it is true winter is here, Michael's toe was broken by a cow, Richard is in the county hospital with an esoteric fever, John's VW was turned-over up on Route 91, Peter's father died last week in Pennsylvania, Pepper is in Rochester waiting for hers to go, the freezer broke down and much of the harvest moved to another house until we can fix it, no storm windows for lack of money and howling winds outside. But it has nothing to do with the city versus the country, it has only to do with the strange twists in our lives which yet excite the attention of the newspapers who display our photographs and write our biographies as professional hippies and postrevolutionaries; and it has to do with Marshall himself, and there will never be another.

Marshall's death was the logical extension of the Concord and Merrimack Rivers trip; indeed, it followed hard on the heels of the boating. Sensitive as he was, he no doubt saw the opportunity to embellish the awfulest October in history and couldn't pass it up; get all the bad shit out of the way, he must have thought, before the new decade begins. What bad angel, thus, has elected to sit over our chimney? When your crop don't fail and your house don't burn down, your best friend will leave you stranded and helpless. Winter will come and snow you in, yet you can't move back to the city despite it because any natural hardship is better than an unnatural life. Every winter the hospitals in Vermont declare dead old men who just one evening neglected to light their stoves.

And here I had the chicken house one-quarter shingled, too, when it happened, and after that Saturday it rained day and night for six days. Everybody stared at each other, each was broken down in his unique way. Nothing got accomplished and yet there was nowhere to go.

Death generates death, then, though we know in our remaining animal instincts that organic material makes carrots grow. It will be a long winter with ghosts behind the walls, and what wise man could be certain that we will make it to the spring? Spring, or life, is always a surprise and a gift, not something we have earned any firm right to.

> It will be long ere the marshes resume,
> It will be long ere the earliest bird,
> So close all the windows and not hear the wind,
> But see all wind-stirred.
>
> —Frost

So the army of corpses, some freshly laid in the ground and others now grown cold and bony, led the people of my country to create a Moratorium, which was nothing more or less than a Memorial Day of the new regime. Didn't Ho Chi Minh have generals? Thus will the Provisional Revolutionary Government have its holidays, and the time of Vietnam will be marked in history books in Skokee, Illinois, as an era of great plague and disaster in the nation. And monuments raised to the great men who "gave their lives" in the service of destroying the old. Marshall wasn't like that, he searched for the life in things, but found it unsatisfactory in the end. He was always taking us down with him, demanding a group involvement in his pain, and he has done it again; and all in the course of living like crazy and kicking up, as John said, a lot of shit for 25 years old.

Was he serious about it or is this just Super-Burn? Will he show up in the cucumber patch next July, and will we say "Marshall, you son of a *bitch"?* Or will this empty numb half-heartedness go on forever, and will we always be sailing the River Styx in our canoe, surveying the damage? Spring is right around the coroner.

*   *   *

From Bow Junction all the way to Plymouth, further north than Thoreau ever managed to get, we jumped from canoe to Volvo as sections of the river gave out underneath us, became too foul to navigate, turned into a bed of high sharp rocks, and trickled weakly through dams and obstructions thrown up by cities like Concord and Manchester, the latter being as one and all recognize the worst city on the planet. We drove to Plymouth at last, determined to find some water worth paddling through, and believing that the Pemigewasset, which runs through that town and becomes the Merrimack just north of Manchester, would still be relatively unspoiled. But in the course of the afternoon's rowing from there down to Ashland, we encountered more rapids alongside a sandbar which, when we sank into it, proved to be quicksand mixed with shit and putrefaction impossible to describe. And we passed a yellow machine engaged in pushing trees into the water and despoiling the air with vast clouds of exhaust, so that even the atmosphere was no longer enjoyable and the sky invisible.

We also discovered that Route 93, which runs from Boston (via a long Detour, of course) up through Lawrence and north, follows the course of the Merrimack exactly, so that no camping spot or island left on the river can be free from the vroom-vroom noises of hell-for-leather diesel trucks and all-night passenger cars tooling up and down the planet bringing people their Pall Malls and Kentucky Bourbon, DDT and mass-produced foam rubber parlor chairs, and a million other things. And these monsters unkindly refused to declare Moratorium since they are not people anyway and thus insensitive to the needs of the living or the demands of the dead. Peter left his car, though, at a place in Ashland or Bridgewater where two bridges crossed the Pemigewasset, one for the railroad and the other for traffic, and we found ourselves all together as night fell on a forest glen in which all the trees were marked with surveyor's identifying paint, signifying that they were scheduled to be bulldozed in the near future. We made the last wood fire that place will know.

The stars were out despite everything and I gave them my thorough uneducated scrutiny (I have never been able to find the Big Dipper, though I can immediately recognize the Northern Lights when they come around in March) as I thought and thought about the war. For the first time I could remember, I felt not the slightest indignity at being punished for an evil I did not create or support. "You get what you pay for," as the fat Texans say. We lived off the destructive energy in Vietnam *even though we were opposed to it,* and now our efforts to find and encourage life are of doubtful promise at best. But we're still alive and trying, and I suppose you are too. Do you suppose it is too late?

Shall we go out and rebuild this thing together? That was on my mind. Will we be able to start anew without nature, with only mankind, to support us? Dresden in ashes was yet potentially a prosperous center for the manufacture of Volkswagens, what will come out of an Atlantic Ocean which casts death and waste on the beaches as well as foam and salt? For lack of anything more overwhelming to tackle, I am willing to try it. At least most of the time. Do you have the strength to join?

Thursday: Ashland, N.H.

Breakfast was hearty and the coffee was strong, so this kid was raring once again to go, though by now with no illusions of having a pleasant or honestly working experience. He longed for his dog, Barf Barf, and thanked whatever stars put him in Vermont for the fact that Mr. B didn't have to drink *this* water. He wondered what the point was in further subjecting his body and soul to such a diseased and hopeless piece of the earth, but pushed these reservations aside to climb into the bow for more of Buzzy's dead-serious lessons in steering. He was not prepared to discover, a full mile from the camping-place, that Peter Simon had lost his wallet somewhere among those doomed trees, with money, driver's license, and Bank Americard; and to eat up a large part of the day in searching the banks for the exact spot in Ashland where we'd camped and then finding the missing papers. God forbid that we should wander the rivers and forests of the planet without our papers in order! Why, friends of mine have been incarcerated for weeks simply for lacking the right papers while passing through Cheyenne, Wyoming. As much as we might philosophically contend that we are free creatures on God's earth, we do not question when a brother says, "Turn around, bow-man, for my driver's license and Bank Americard."

Great confusion now ensued as we considered which way to go: north to the White Mountain National Forest, south to Concord again, east to Portsmouth, west to Vermont? It hardly made any difference, we'd so badly botched up Thoreau's itinerary by then, and so much of the original waters were now inaccessible to living creatures. The question was resolved by paddling back to where we had left Peter's car so he could drive to Plymouth and watch the Mets win their Series. Somebody hit a homer and somebody else got hit by a pitch. I imagined our party in a Camel ad (we'd paddle a mile etc.) and loudly said, "You other guys, *start walkin'.*" We fooled around in Bridgewater, Ashland, and Holderness until we found a small tributary which led us to a stand of virgin pine holding out majestically in full view of an abandoned homestead and a railroad trestle. Buzzy guessed that the pine was on too great a pitch to be of use to 1930 American lumbering equipment, but in this nuclear age, we knew, it would not long go on rising. I hugged one of the trees and could not hardly stretch my arms around it.

With all the time lost in wallets and such, darkness seemed to fall inordinately early, but of course we were approaching the solstice with every day and might have expected as much. While I was in the cities, I lived by night and slept all day, for the streets of town were always more bearable under thin cover of grey; their lights made it easy to walk, and all the enclosed spaces were brightly lit with fraudulent sunshine, so I had the *impression* that I was alive. In the woods, though, nightfall is literally the end of the day. The degree to which you may perform outdoor chores depends on variables like the temperature, the moon, and the stars. You *must* make your hay while the sun shines. It terrifies me at times, so ill-adjusted am I to progress, to think that these very terms (names for the planets and stars) are just about obsolete in the day-to-day language of working people in Manchester and Lowell, professional people in L.A. and Paris, even Greenhouse Farmers in Pennsylvania.

The waning hours of afternoon also brought rain; and, disgusted, we set out in the car for . . . somewhere. The conversation in the back seat was in the quiet tones you can imagine defeated football players using after the big game. Buzzy spoke of real rivers he had sailed, most of them outside the United States; and I protested mildly that Vermont was still OK, then wondered how long it would take for my words to be ready-to-eat. The general talk rested on the subject of expatriation, the hows and wheres of it I mean. I imagined a family in Greenland taking in Verandah and me as "refugees from America"; it would not be an extraordinary scene in history. National boundaries mean nothing in the New Age, of course, and all we know of American history would make us anxious to leave, were the genuine natives not so thoroughly destroyed and the prospect of finding an untarnished culture and geography so dismal. Besides, our leaving would be the same as our staying, just the shifting of bodies from one spot to another on the big checkerboard, and the land never noticing.

And that's where the story ends I suppose, with the land, though the trip ended in Dr. Gus Dodge's house in Portsmouth, with Peter getting injected with gamma globulin as protection against Merrimack hepatitis. (As a Merrimack native, I am immune.) The land at the farm, at this writing, is alive and well if soaked with rain. It stretches out as far as my eyes can see, forming exquisite perspectives on all sides and limited only by the open sky which protects it. It generates new life at a furious pace, such that our main problem is keeping the forest from reclaiming itself; trees, saplings, grass, hay, vegetables, spices, flowers, and weeds crop up in riotous confusion, making oxygen and protein for deer, muskrats, coons, owls, porcupines, skunks, bobcats, snakes, goats, cows, horses, honeybees, rabbits, mice, cats, dogs, and people and a million other fine fellows and gals great and small. "Live off the land," our fathers said, and so we do. They didn't tell us to live in groups, they preferred the lonely family circle, so we have rejected that part. They didn't care enough about living off the rivers, oceans, and skies. We'll eat no meat or fish, it is clear. We'll burn no oil or gases in our houses, and finally in our cars. We'll bury our organic waste as deep as we can. We'll try to stay alive, for what else can we do? Friend, we are barking up the right trees.

*   *   *

Henry concludes in his *Week:*

My friend is not of some other race or family of men, but flesh of my flesh, bone of my bone. He is my real brother. I see his nature groping yonder so like mine. We do not live far apart. Have not the fates associated us in many ways? It says in the Vishnu Purana: "Seven paces together is sufficient for the friendship of the virtuous, but thou and I have dwelt together." Is it of no significance that we have so long partaken of the same loaf, drank at the same fountain, breathed the same air summer and winter, felt the same heat and cold; that the same fruits have been pleased to refresh us both, and we have never had a thought of different fiber the one from the other!

As surely as the sunset in my latest November shall translate me to the ethereal world, and remind me of the ruddy morning of youth; as surely as the last strain of music which falls on my decaying ear shall make age to be forgotten, or, in short, the manifold influences of nature survive during the term of our natural life, so surely my Friend shall forever be my Friend, and reflect a ray of God to me, and time shall foster and adorn and consecrate our Friendship, no less than the ruins of temples. As I love nature, as I love singing birds, and gleaming stubble, and flowing rivers, and morning and evening, and summer and winter, I love thee, my Friend.

—November, 1969.

Letter from a Foreign City

to CMG

Gentle in the lap of love,
the bed, board and body
of the man more to my liking,
reclining in the quilts of morning,
I am writing for some fatherly advice.

I have redeemed my days,
have peeled your life from mine
like a tangerine,
and go about the kitchen
free and graceful as a newlywed
seasoning the eggs,
like a virgin seasoning eggs for the first time.

And yet,
my nights are twisted
with the image of you
riding swift as a thief,
riding west with my sanity

captured in a great sack,
my heart kicking and pounding
like a ravished waif
with the image
of your fingers fastened to my body
like electrodes
plotting the score of my womanhood
on a lie detector.

Or the evening truce
between venom and boredom
when we curled together
innocent and happy
as a pair of socks
fresh from the washer,
the chambers of our hearts,
adjoining rooms,
a suite, a minuet.

The nights you loved me
ruffled in my sleep
have left their mark.
I say you ruined me.

I spin my days
on an empty spool
as a careful seamstress
ripping a hem
rewinds the thread
to sew again—

the thread
so fragile, scarce, and dear,
to love is crazy.

Say why
when you cradle her
to sleep,
it looks so easy.

—Verandah Porche

2. WiNTER:
The Eye Don't Lie

For Ellen Snyder, who knows my secret.

A good artist is a deadly enemy of society; and the most dangerous thing that can happen to an enemy, no matter how cynical, is to become a beneficiary. No society, no matter how good, could be mature enough to support a real artist without mortal danger to that artist. Only no one need worry: for this same good artist is about the one sort of human being who can be trusted to take care of himself.

—James Agee, 1939
Let Us Now Praise Famous Men

Omnia vincit amor

I. Tight and Quick

When winter came, it was barely noticeable to us. Though the planet was dying before us, our private world had so long been dead that the weather stopped happening to us, became a matter of small concern and small talk. This sudden and unexpected alienation from the environment proved to be the hardest blow of all, and we began to talk of California.

Some nights before, I dreamed my father had died. It was early morning, 3 or 4 A.M., and I walked down the dark streets of South Lawrence to the Irish funeral home where I knew my father would lie. I passed the sporting-goods store, the bicycle-repair shop, the podiatrist who recommended Epsom Salts, the pharmacy where youth pined away with desire over raspberry rootbeer, the candy store where bets were taken, the florist who donated flowers to the church on Christmas and Easter, the florid Irish church itself where Mary is annually Queen of South Broadway, then the funeral "home," or "parlor"—our society's vision of a model home, carpets all clean and draperies lush, quiet enough to hear a pin drop as the nuns would say, this is it: a final resting place different from the fish and chips kitchens and dark oil-heated bedrooms where children crammed and life went on. The undertaker, in my dream, had a teenage son ("teenage" rather than young, I too was much older then) all pimples and ducktail though this was the present day to be sure, and he passed me with a sneer, girlfriend (Doris? Patty? Sheila?) on arm, and the undertaker himself descended a vast spiraling staircase dressed in what is commonly called "evening wear" by those who know no night, and he smiled coyly at me and wrapped his freckled hand around my stooped shoulder. "Is it true?" I cried. "Don't worry lad," he answered, "just go to California."

Though I know the arguments about the Indians and I feel myself no native to this place, I am an American, which is to say a Booger, and how could I help going to California for relief of weary heart, how refuse the lifetime barrage of assurance that it's always summer there, how doubt that a change of place would bring in its course a change of psychic season? Millions of Americans are going, going, going to California every day of the year, my friend Dan said it this way: the continent is tilted to the West and everybody who isn't *rooted down* is sliding to California. Tumbling to California. O they claim to go for the sunlight though they know it's covered with smog, for the ocean they know is shiny with petroleum which took millions of years to grow underground in Oklahoma and only yesterday to run out completely, for their *health,* for *retirement;* when they actually seek *engagement,* a place under the sun in the growing cast of the greatest movie ever made, the most extreme evolution of the American psychology, the *furthest-out.* Like suicidal seers, we are going, going, going off the deep end.

I had a friend who went crazy. The truth, for him, was too hard to bear. On a certain morning he merely said, "Take me to the hospital, I must go to the hospital," and though it was wrong and we did him no good to remove him from the Whole World we had to deal with, it was also in the city and many years ago; and so we took him. Just so with the many bodies racing across the planet headed for the Apocalypse, they know they are going to madness, they want to be in a safe place to go mad, they cannot lose a moment, it may be soon too late; so they undertake to bridge the great deserts, scale the biggest bumps, suffer the long, long prairie and fight tooth and nail the flat plateau of the middle; they save all their lives, putting away for tomorrow what they can only use today (it doesn't keep); no explanation is required, none makes sense; and though we know it's wrong we let them let go, even today.

"You'll feel better once you get in the hospital, they have people who can *take care of you* there."

"Sometimes I've seen people, though, that it *did a lot of good.*"

Are you still with me? We are going to California because we are going, we've been there before but we left something behind, besides it's winter and'll be warm there (there's always an excuse), we are in it together so don't try to back out later, leave the room right now if your heart ain't in it. I am a part of you, and we're nothing special; I would not exist without your picking up this and granting me life. Feel free to claim me as a dependent on your tax form. I am, after all, your brother, and live under your roof.

Let's wait till Christmas because Christmas in Vermont is fondly remembered as a moment of high energy and good vibrations, of which we are sorely in need. You will make me a blue California Shirt with golden cuffs and open throat, loose and light, when I am faced (but how could you know?) with the necessity of being tight and quick. I will draw you a picture, write you a poem, bake you a cake. We'll have an orgy of giving without the benefit of Macy's or Sears. And together, we'll cut down a tree in the deep forest, always killing for our sport it seems, but we'll make it a small tree as if the young don't matter like the old, and the size of our sin looks diminished in the brief light of our living room; and decorate it the night before Christmas with popcorn and cranberries; and float a hand-made star of the East over it; and wish, in our curious way that forbids saying-so, peace and goodwill to men and women and all critters that scarf on our ground. May they say of me when I go to the other side: "Christ was OK in his Book."

We are young, and have time for Christmas in Vermont before we have to go to California; we are young and have time to do most anything we want to do; we are unemployed and hard at play. We have time, and time is money, so we're rich. All the poor people see us in our beat-up cars and torn clothing, know we heat with wood and not strange subterranean poisons, and turn to their children saying, "O, those people, they are rich." They want what we've got, and we want them to have it. I want *you* to be rich, too. Sun in the morning and the moon at night, as the old song goes, and all the time in between—that's my Christmas gift to you. Take these things into your own back-yard, and don't let them go. *Never work, never worry* —at least as an ideal. Welcome to the New Age.

I am being altogether too simple, and these thoughts are common, obvious, and dare I say it, natural. But we are common creatures, you and I, and so our lofty expectations cannot be disappointed. We *ain't* looking for Oxford footnotes or "new politics" or any other shuffling of matter from here to there; no, not really; we'd be satisfied with loving each other, just us a coupla dogs, as Marty said. Who among us wouldn't rather be in love than be in America?

I am thus no prophet, philosopher, or poet, not at least in the academic senses, I am simply that half of you which is crazy and footloose, a mad young man in America. And I'm taking you for a ride.

It hadn't snowed much before Christmas in Vermont, you know it's different every year, and folks were talking of Open Winter, that means you don't have to struggle with your life on the line to get to a pack of cigarettes, you can simply *drive to town;* but on Christmas itself it began to snow a snow that didn't quit for five days and left five feet behind. Everything you forgot to bring in got lost till April under the planet's new petticoat, and locomotion by all but skis (never use 'em myself) became difficult if not impossible; and so any thought we might have had of tarrying a day or two before leaving became unthinkable. We were on the road after how many hours of quiet and warmth in the womb of our farmhouse, me 'n' Michael 'n' Dale in M's swift Peugot, 1964 404 *Sedan,* which goes by the name of Amazing Grace and boasts a hand-crank which flips 'er over when no battery charger will serve, and the only outlets open sky and space. In the dark, in the cold, in the face of the great storm, we backed away from the barn and left the shed in our winter's dust and only looked back once to see the noses pressed against windowpanes, hands limply waving goodbye, some saying, in the long shadow of Bloom's grave, they'll never be back, this is the last time we'll see those lovers on the planet.

And they were right to say so, for each of us knows somebody who went to California and was never seen again.

Instantly, we were pitched into the measure and rhythm of our journey. Now is no time for easy smiling or checkerboard leisure, now is no time for whatever we want to do, for the great race has begun and will not soon be over—not until we have made the other side and returned home again to spin our yarns. This is no Melville saga, though, or anything culled from dusty bookshelves out of our past, this is happening now and we are only the tiniest fraction of the energy being spent right now in pursuit of the West Coast, or W. C., or Asylum, or whatever. The roads between our house and the border of Massachusetts are unpaved and sometimes unplowed, murder on the cars and thus of course sacred to the peace and goodwill of the people; and at the border of Massachusetts our insignificant road, too little to boast a number and barely two-cars wide, ungraced by commerce of any measure and no artery for mass-produced goods to anybody, at the border this winding breezy twisting bulging road becomes paved, right out there in the middle of nowhere some great Taxman has put an asphalt surface inimical to all life, hard and unyielding to the fragile April bursts of weed and flower and tree, a road on which nothing not only grows but will never. And that is invariably my first impression of Massachusetts when I go down there, that the path which shocks and tumbles my Volkswagen and sends the dogs bumping into the back seat, turns into solid footing for valves and pistons and Goodyear tires though it is not Boston or Worcester or even Springfield and everything but people lives there. The dirt roads of Vermont are warm and reassuring even in the worst of weather, and when we skidded we were actually floating on them, the trees and banks on both sides serving as our protective insulation, and even if we skidded off the road, we knew, the worst that could happen would be we'd end up in a ditch, up a creek, or over a bridge in Vermont, and there'd surely be some way of working with it, solving it. I have seen legions of the mad paranoid gain security and self-confidence merely by staying in Vermont for a while, and I know one or two who dare not venture out of it; they are *safe* here not like in New York, New Hampshire, Massachusetts, places where bad burly men may ask for your license and registration, or worse, search your naked body and demean your dignity for no reason better than bad vibrations. "Where *do* bad vibrations come from, Raymond?" Johnny asked me last night, and I had no answer. But the point is though it's long established Vermont is a place of strong white magick, a place friendly to adventurers of the mind and body, a holy place, though we and thousands of others know this and never take it for granted, yet we must risk the relatively inferior terrain and vibration of Massachusetts and points south and west, and the huge strain of friendless middle America, the lonely gargantua with not so much as a single true playmate, in order to reach that other magnetic pole, that California which shows magick can, too, be black. Vermont belongs to The Band, California to the Rolling Stones, at least now; and now is all the time we know.

My mother often said: "Don't go looking for trouble, it'll come right to your door." She never told me what to do once it arrived, so I merely reverse the axiom. This story is full of axioms, lessons we've learned together, yet we make the same mistakes again, and again.

Michael and Dale and me were huddled in Grace's front seat gathering what false heat we could from her failing hot-air blower, no cousin to the Ashley Automatic ("Burn Wood—Live Modern") that strokes our numb coldness with waves of delicious brute energy till we fall asleep. Sleep was not in sight for us and though we were tired & confused we kept going, once out of Vermont, hell for leather across the little plains of Massachusetts now blown treacherous and slick with snow, with precipitation from the sky which seems our enemy down there, God's revenge on the commonwealth perhaps for her many sins. Christ died for 'em, after all. We knew we could trust the faithful caravans of state highway trucks in civilized down-there to scrape the roads for us, aware as they are more of the dangers the snow brings than the beauty it *is,* we could trust the good people of that place to dispatch God's wrath to the gutters and sewerage systems and out of their way (for there are some, in this day and age, who throw beer cans in the forest and walk away thinking they've gotten *rid* of them); but our faith was, blessedly, abused and nobody came to silence the tumult in the heavens; and Massachusetts was even more a forsaken and Arctic place than Vermont had been hours earlier; and we were alone in her.

It was a night unfit for man or machine. We were undergoing what proved to be a recurring theme in the group mind—: don't look back, we can't turn around now, the road is closed, the bridges behind us are burning: the snow getting deeper and old Route 2 harder to discern through the half-defrosted windscreen, we were the only life in Massachusetts, six legs covered with an Irish blanket and three heads shrouded by pull-over knit caps, thirty idle fingers encrusted in gloves, we were life suspended in our time-capsule, three bodies and minds ready and able to swing into action but saving the big freak-out for the end of the road, for the nonce all taut and wide-eyed with fear and trembling for our lives. Could Amazing Grace deliver us unto the arms of Boston when no other fiery clunkbeast dared venture out in this night?

What are these adventures compared to Byrd's expedition to the North Pole, crossing the Himalayas, or any true miracle such as giving or accepting birth? Nothing, clearly, to the great material accomplishments of our race, but that is because our ecstatic adventure, the frontier we cross daily, is no untamed forest or turgid river, but the tricky loose sands of the mind.

> Bless you, my heart.
> The shell bangles slip
> from my wasting hands.
> My eyes, sleepless for days,
> are muddied.
>> Get up, let's go, let's get out
>> of this loneliness here.
>
> Let's go
> where the tribes wear
> the narcotic wreaths of *cannabis*
> beyond the land of Katti,
> the chieftain with many spears,
>> let's go, I say,
>> to where my man is,
>>
>> enduring even
>> alien languages.
>>>> Malmulanar, *Kur* ll
>>>> Second Century, B.C.

You know what we have to do: to conquer the roads to be sure, and find the tribes and the dope which will loosen our tongues and minds, but also to reveal our secrets. Verandah says I have secrets which even *I* don't know about, how then shall I strip naked to Michael, to Dale, to you? Would I be worth your time if I were less than naked? No no. But that is *my* problem here, and my anguish later if I have failed or betrayed you in any way. I am writing this by night in late winter, by day I screw holes in maple trees the better to catch their energy and spill their sap, the first pulpy splash exactly the color and consistency of good old-fashioned mancome; " 'twas ever thus." It doesn't hurt the trees, they say, but then who knows what hurts a tree? And I am masturbating here for you, will it hurt me? It is certainly a more indirect way of making love than if you and I could somehow find our way to a big round bed together; but we know the seed I am spilling by day and night, on the ground and into your mind, cannot be totally wasted, contributes its share toward supporting our endless lives.

We stopped twice.

We pulled into the town of Montague, Massachusetts, to see our chums at the farm there; there are farms everywhere now, and we might go in any direction on the compass to find warm bread and salt, but these Montagnards are flesh of our bones so to speak and whenever we are in Massachusetts we go there to play rough. Steve Diamond had told me at the Sagittarian Bash, among other things, that we played rough, and so we decided to rough him up a bit and took the fork off the impassable highway onto the impossible road to Montague and caught him at 5 A.M., closing hour of the Owls' Club, which only meets in winter when there's Nothing To Do. "We're going to California, Stevie, and there's room for *you*." "When?" "Right now!" "Give me a minute to get packed." What will he need? Steve, you will need your headband to keep your hair from weighing down your head, better bring Agee and Crowley and Vonnegut, you will need to let go all the fine and honest things you have here, need an open heart, need to be crazy. He was, alas, just a smidgeon too sane. He would at first go all the way to California, then only to Nashville where the Kool Kats jive, then just as far as Boston, then not beyond the limits of the Owls' Club. Johnny Wilton, that erudite editor of *Green Mountain Post,* a magazine which cannot be properly said to exist, was too comfortably tucked under his quilts and the dog Black Booger (who speaks with the voice of Taj Mahal) all settled down for the night, for either of them to budge, much less tumble, to California; they are no fools, and though Bloom haunts the castle it's still the best place to hibernate when the days grow short and all but the wind ceases to speak.

We stopped a second time at a diner on Route 2, drinking coffee to exacerbate our already nervous psyches, hearing tall tales of strong men (truckers, we guessed) who wouldn't venture out into the storm and swore on lifetimes of experience "working" this path that Boston could never be reached until the infernal blizzard stopped. Boston, that you could slide into like a depression almost anytime your head was so badly fractured, had become the unattainable summit!

But "the superior man," as the *I Ching* says, pays no heed to false counsel and indeed you can't rely on Americans these days to give you road or weather advice based on common sense; rather, you must filter and temper the advice of all strangers through some levels of consciousness-consideration—viz., poor means rich, filthy means spotless, impossible often means difficult at worst. Naturally, too, there are some whose standards of possibility, convenience, and comfort are even more exaggerated than our own—the wandering freaks who insist it's easy to milk 40 cows a day and make $6,000 a year while working only two hours daily, etc. We paid no heed to the sure doom we'd been forewarned of, just as we refuse, these days, to listen to negative vibrations of any kind; for us, everything is possible; if the heart is willing what ecstatic adventure is too risky? *What is risk?* But the truckers were not lying, and for them—who were neither young nor burdened with death, illness, winter, and madness—for them Boston was beyond the pale and unapproachable. For us, nothing could have been worse than not-getting there, and no hoops of fire too scorching for Asbestos Kids hot to trot.

> Trot, trot to Boston,
> Jiggety-jig,
> Home again, home again,
> Quick like a pyg!
> —(Old Song)

With dispatch, then, we struggled into Boston over a sea of treacherous foam, proof again if we needed it that Christmas for most folks has become the inverse of what it purports to be, pain and wretchedness and loneliness rather than peace and goodwill, and that we were not, really, exempt from this blasphemy as we flattered ourselves to be—not at least outside the boundaries of good Vermont. We made the entire trip in about three times our normal time, still much faster than any trot I suppose, in Amazing Grace whose sheer dogged usefulness nearly excuses her consumption of Esso and Oilzum ("good" mileage at 35 to a *gallon* and who knows how many gallons over how many roads). No secrets had been revealed, for the heart's inner-mosties are content to stay put when the body itself is in peril and we'd concentrated mostly on staying awake and small talk ("Michael, watch out for that mountain!") and, without "benefit" of amphetamines (which make you bite your teeth on the down part, crunchy like the packed snow in December), we were too pooped to pucker.

We sought out the home offices of the Driveaway Company, struggling for traction on the main boulevards of Boston, for we knew the friendly Driveaway Man (so mobile is our family, and so often have these trips been necessary, that we expend some energy keeping on good terms with the Man) would have a car for us, a swift sharp Cougar Sting Ray Booger Car in which we could tearass across country like the fastest and coldest of the fellow mad. Why subject such a warm friend as Amazing Grace to the hardships we ourselves would go through, when we could beat shit out of some other guy's new chariot, put the 3 grand miles on *his* Firestones, blow *his* radiator, with his full advice and consent? So we went to the Driveaway company and talked to the slick man who wore sideburns and talked so closely to his telephone that it seemed to me he was sucking it off; and we looked at him Sanpaku; we were tired & confused and would sign anything to get a heated nuthouse bound for California; and so did not object to boarding one bound for Albuquerque, New Mexico, which I reasoned is so far out there it's *practically* California, nor to the fact it was full of the owner's toys, nor to the promise that we'd surely be able to get another car out of Albuquerque. They took our pictures, then, and made us the lucky if temporary owners of a 1969 Ford Fairlane Station Wagon with polyethylene seats, padded plastic dashboard, gauges and dials to sparkling distraction, standard transmission, insurance, bills of lading, owner's name and address in New Mexico, and a printed warning of sure federal prosecution if we delayed delivery of this blob tucked safely in the glove compartment. The Driveaway Man said don't drive it today though fellows wait for the storm to end, so we drove Grace down to the waterfront, though you can't see it, to our friend Dug's house and there collapsed into fitful and overheated sleep.

When I awoke, it was night; you can always tell when it is night in the city. Night there is evil, and sure enough hell itself was outside my window, sure enough the warehouse dockside building across the street from dug's high-ceilinged studio was burning down and sirens screaming, flames rising as from the Atlantic itself. I remembered the oil slicks off Santa Barbara and wondered if we were jumping from the frying pan, etc. etc. It was night, who knows what time for there is no sun by which to gauge the hour and the moon is hidden over the roof, and I was safely tucked into dug's spare sleeping bag and watching the Atlantic burn down; not a good omen, I thought, for the weeks ahead. Dug's place is built over a restaurant which he designed, where it costs 65 dollars for four people to fill their gelatin tummies, but Dug don't own the restaurant so I couldn't be angry with him for its decadence; and living on *top* of it ain't a bad trip at all. I awoke and smelled cooking from the kitchen, and remembered everything; I made ready to wake each day now in a strange and exotic surrounding, after so many days, nearly years, of waking to my own blue jays and peepfrogs and near my own outhouse. First things first, did Dug have any dope? Yessir, yessir, three bags full; all of us had it I suppose, it wasn't Dug's dope but it's the only thing, except money, that grows on trees in the cities and of course because who could live there without it? Just name me one person who could live there without some kind of mindfucking Forget pill ingested daily, or seven times daily, pills and smokes, tokes and needles, tabs and hits that are fun & instructive to take anywhere, but addicting only in Boston. We passed the piece pipe and broke down over pepperoni, salad, cereals, coffee, cognac, and anise. The storm was in its second day, still going strong, and the ocean was burning across the street. We "put on" the Beatles (*Abbey Road*) to drown out the commotion from the street, we were like aristocrats shutting off the rumbling rabble below our balcony, and that's how Kitty Genovese died I suppose, so many people heard her screams but they couldn't cope with it and put on the Beatles instead. "Because the world is round, it turns me on/Because the wind is high, it blows my mind/Because the sky is blue, it makes me cry." These lovely if somewhat saccharine sentiments pouring through KLH Bellbottom Special System, recorded in Fleet Street Studio, on sale at E. J. Korvette's, packaged Nature (just like this book) & good for something: for helping you not cope. Because a whole lot of the time you can't.

Dug is our dear friend who had the urge to become an Artist and so thoroughly did that he became capable of supporting himself by his work and that's where trouble starts; but he is wise enough to see how his time is all bought up these last years and he's working too hard and not taking any chances any more—as he once did when we crackled together in of all places college—so he says Take Me Down to California Baby and poof goes the 65 dollar Restaurant, the job, the shoe store in Worcester, and the Big D on his name, and a new dug was born! Now it's Michael 'n' Dale 'n' *dug* 'n' me in the Ford Fairlane Leopard, and we decided though it's dark and snowing there's no time like the present so let's go, and for the first time I knew we were really doing it, because we were zooming in the lizzard toward New York City now and I never go there at all unless my life is in pieces.

When you are undertaking a massive chore, say driving 10,000 miles in a month or writing a book on some sort of, even if self-imposed, deadline, all your consolations are rational and thus easily demolished; chiefly, you must remind yourself that every little bit adds up and by all means avoid looking at your enterprise in its entirety until it is finished, when likely as not you'll decide it wasn't worth all that energy. I can't think of anything more psychically wearing than the drive across America, and that is why I did it—because the boogers living in my head needed to be cleared out by a good shot of pain and worry over simpler things than sexual inadequacy and suicide. Drive, the man said, until your asshole wears out from polyethylene buggery, keep those uniformly printed green interstate directional signs stacked in your mind like a deck of solitaire cards to be laid one upon another, game after game, till you get four kings up and every mystery unraveled. When you can put "San Francisco" on top of "Palo Alto," you've earned a week's rest. Drive till you don't know whether you're running from or to something, or why, and don't care to find out. And in the hard, hard isolation of your car, with your friends, ask favors and make remarks that'd be unforgivable in any other context and'll be forgotten and dismissed two weeks after you're off the road. Eat Meat, it gives you that rough 'n' readiness for *working on out;* drink coffee, as if it could thwart your sleeping, your dreams out of control; talk of small and great issues, the past, the future, talk of anything for it will help *kill time* in this suspended universe, and talking is beginning and end of our range of possible activity while time is dying.

Michael was at the wheel, for he drove with more confidence and skill than any of the rest of us, having been a wildass kid in Oregon. His hair was long, curly, black, his mustache drooping Fu Manchu, o a splendid billboard hippie he looked in those days, his face hardly visible but for the wide round eyes that coat and stroke you with Scorpio Scorpio Rising, born of Scorpio Scorpio Rising high-energy knew-that-before-you-said-so vibrations. He has as fine and upstanding a past as you'd want, the family went West to make their fortune, there's an old grandmother with an American fictionbook name, mother a woman of no mean sensitivity to apocalyptic acts and ideas, three sisters; a man among women. Father so great he's dead. Everybody loves Michael, everybody wants Michael in one way or other, his mind or body or soul, it must be hard for him sometimes.

Dale rode shotgun. Jewish cowgirl, sister, mother, daughter, on the moment you meet her she's one of the reg'lars, tight & quick, highly competent, independent; later you know she's a lost orphan, too, we're babies that fell out of our prams when nannies' backs were turned, she's physical and knows the arts and intricacies of love by her heart. And makes a word stand for a whole rainbow of conceptions; and a rainbow on canvas or paper in place of a million words. And she melts quick, catch her or she'll disappear. She's from Brooklyn, knows the score there so she's here, father an old salt ex-Navy officer school of hard knocks, etc., and she went to City College and taught smackscene grammar school but only for a year, that was enough. Properly called "Missie Dale" and other endearing femininity numbers, and properly dressed in long pseudofur coat and brown dowdy hat with feather. Wholesome and infinitely deep, no matter how far in you go there's more of her, and every moment a new and startling revelation.

Dug shared backseat with me. Dug puts idea on paper, canvas, accordion key, wall, or just across your mind and it's etched, it's clean and precise and exquisite. Throws no curves. Knows, knows, knows. One of most Wanted Artists out there in great world of commerce for which he has no mind. Fat, jolly, substantial not flabby, laughs and world laughs with 'im, etc., but it's important to see this: dug as unpretentious unpretending humble fellow of goodwill, Mr. Natural, mindreader and bringer of both peace and plenty. Thus the superior man. No sexual image to my blurred mind, rather the cosmic psychic force; yet clearly emanating yes do it it's OK sex-energy from each pore. Dug as Falstaff, Hamlet, Emerson, father, uncle, brother, who cannot be profaned because his whole body is in search of sanctity.

Me in back seat. Me. Me. Me. Who me? Catalyst and funnel for energy and ideas of others, brought together in perhaps unlikely combinations, through but not *by* me. No more me.

*   *   *

Mantra for Vernal Equinox
Equinox:
  sticks in box:
    no more cold.
  sticks in box:
    no more cold.
Nice Big Dog.

The sticks-in-box began as wood in the stove; chuck your sticks right in that box (Ashley Automatic, Reeves-Dover, or whatever) and soon, though not immediately, there will be no more cold. Just so with men and women, men and men, women and women, dogs, all life on the planet: by making love we fulfill our need to invest in the future, we make children or perhaps only ourselves. "Sticks in box, no more cold." Nice Big Dog is Mamoushka, the Russian lady dawg who visits us and this morning came in to keep us warm while we threw sticks in the box. Winter remains a while and the wind is both cold and bitter—nothing stops the wind—but spring and rebirth are clearly with us as well.

* * *

Here we go in earnest now, the trip between Boston and New York City (do-wah-do-wah-do-wah-diddy): it must have been the most extraordinary excursion on those roads in recent history for though it was night and traffic should have been sparse, we encountered not a single other car the entire length of the route. All the millions who live between these two great metropoli had seemingly given up on the three-day-old storm, and even the impressive, expensive Merritt Parkway, which links Massachusetts with New York State for 45 cents, was unplowed and unfriendly. Christmas fell on a Thursday, by now it was Saturday, so the inescapable week-weekend dichotomy (which even we unemployed cannot escape, for our guests from the city nearly always descend during the Friday-night-to-Sunday-night time slot) was also in force; and surely the peaceable folk of New Canaan, Conn., had concluded that nothing whatever could be done with the storm, best to ignore it till it's over. I cannot recall exactly why, but I was chosen to drive us most of this route into New Jersey, and I remember feeling distinctly unworthy of the responsibility involved in guiding three such precious lives, as well as my own, through that terrifying darkness. The super Ford did its stuff, as it was manufactured to do for two or three years before breaking down, part by greasy part, until it would ineluctably die and be traded in for another; and begin its *real* station in this life, oxidizing away at an agonizingly slow rate, making a junkyard out of what was once a pasture. But at 1-year-old it was already, I knew, suspect and untrustworthy, and so I paid especial psychic debts to all of its operative motor-driven parts out of fear—based on experience—that one or more of them would simply stop working, we'd be without lights, or wipers, or carburetor, or else the automatic choke would flood the engine or the power brakes fail to stop the thing or the warrantied tires blow out for no good reason.

I carried all these anxieties through the four states of mind— Massachusetts, Connecticut, New York, New Jersey—like an old-fashioned Jewish mother; and faithfully delivered my charges unto the gates of Trenton, there relinquishing control over the fates to trusty Mike and retiring to fitful acidic bouts of sleeping in the back seat. Neither Dale nor dug "drives," that is they own no operator's permit and are thus free of a whole world of aggravations and burdens that've been dragging me under for maybe seven, eight years now. Dale asked me to teach her to drive once and we did that number for a couple of lessons until we nearly hit some innocent pedestrians on a lonely country road and I said "O Christ" and gave it up figuring (and I can't really explain this) the day is nigh upon us when *nobody* will have to drive and we'll all be safer and sounder for it; teaching Dale to drive was like teaching her to smoke cigarettes or something, it was impossibly reactionary and thoroughly Wrong, I was doing her no good by it; and if the future drivingless society incorporates robot-controlled cars or Big Brother cars or some other form of cleaner engine and freedom from responsibility for the *individual,* if that happens why by all likelihoods we'll be walking or just staying home all the time anyway. So fuck it, sez I, my number with internal-combustion engines is rapidly reaching its denouement, I've already cut back on driving to the point at which I seriously consider, before setting out on any road, is the likelihood of a good time at my destination sufficient to overcome the rotten karmic damage of getting there, and if the answer isn't clearly yes, I walk to the sugarbush instead.

So much of the process of becoming free in my country, it seems, is in withdrawing from all the awful things we've been deliberately and systematically taught to need—everything from additives in the food to a car for every really "independent" person; so that a good deal of our manner and program must be negative rather than positive. We are the folks who *do not do* all those corrupt things, etc. etc. But the positive, new, and forward aspects of the life are coming on strong now, and will exonerate us in the long run, I'm sure, from any accusation that we merely drew back without pushing upward as well.

It was even in bleak New Jersey, then, that I turned the reins over to M and quit driving, as it turned out, for the entire remainder of the journey. We got into N. J. from N. Y. by the most conventional and heavily trafficked route, the space machine wonder of the George Washington Bridge, even which had got into the spirit and was nearly bereft of traffic. New Jersey was hardly worth stopping-in for reasons which are almost so universally known as to be consensus; New Jersey, in our Newleft paranoid fantasy days, was the place wherein all the political powers of the '60's would be exiled and made to remain forever; a place so depressing, smelly, ugly, and utterly without charm that I cannot even get into describing it. (Naturally, there are "nice" parts, or so I'm told, but the major public roads there display only the foulest shit on the East Coast, so the pleasures of the good Jersey must perforce be abated by the bad taste acquired in *getting* there.) We took the sunrise in a land of smokestacks and swamp and headed directly into Pennsylvania, home of the Dutch.

Being now very hungry and tired and having eaten nothing whatever since Boston, we stopped at a restaurant off the Pennsy Turnpike which advertised itself in dozens of lurid billboards as the best goddamn Dutch cooking in the area and if you didn't believe it well you just ought to stop there and try it. We lurched into the parallel parking lot and nodded at the papier-maché Pa Dutchman, who dipped his head and repeated through crackling sound-system imperfections that we were welcome and thanks for coming. The food was overpriced, underparceled, and in general common as dirt, and the atmosphere one of quite honestly incredible carnivalesque, and if the Pennsylvania Dutch farmers really ate like that, I don't wonder they are going extinct. What was most astonishing, though, was the palpable obviousness of the burn—like anybody with better than a day's experience wandering the planet could see this joint was thrown up with plastic overnight and could afford to burn its patrons blind seeing as how most of them would never be back this way again. The arrogance with which the management was shoving all these greasy eggs down our throats, and the coldness with which we were dealt, convinced us too to try just as hard as we might to not eat in restaurants at all during this trip, to buy food in markets where we could and munch it in the hog, rather than sit there freaking out over the desolation and miserable fare and vibration.

We tore out again headed for Nashville, which I believed could not be so many miles away, for it was in Nashville alone that we could sleep in real beds in a real person's real home, and we had neither the money for nor the capacity to tolerate a motel. But the warrantied tire blew out for no good reason in the middle of a very long, very high, very narrow bridge, while snow flew mad & fast around us; so we bumped and grinded to the end of the bridge holding breaths against the likelihood of ruining the rim, then found that the road bended sharply to the right just after the bridge, and that the pull-over or emergency lane was packed six feet deep with plowed snow. But there was no choice so we stopped and died momently with each swift boogercar that missed killing us by inches until the Highway Dept. came by and put up flares; we discovered that the blowout for no reason happened on the right side of the car, now flush with a hard & vertical snowbank, and dug out that bank with our fingers and a piece of cardboard, working against sure destruction; then learned that the spare tire was buried under the Ford owner's incredible heap of toys, and so laid his cameras, Samsonite luggage, blankets, and tools all over the Pennsy Turnpike in order to reach it; then raced away and spent all day, All Day, in Carlisle, Pa., ped-xing the Firestone warranty guy to sell us a new tire (the blowout was 1 month old and utterly unsalvageable), got the word as to how Nashville was unreachable, nobody would go out in this storm, couldn't even make it to the Virginia border, and left in a cloud of determined despair.

And so on. Virginia, Maryland, and West Virginia passed us by in the dark and storm, the sun set and rose again, and then there was Tennessee—"greenest state in the land of the free" according to Disney. Hadn't a been for Jason, etc. Sing now the song of the South:

You will wake up some morning and find yourself in the South. The South! But why? The South has nothing to do with anything, nobody you really love lives in the South, nothing you need comes from the South, you have identified with *Easy Rider* and centuries before that Goodman, Chaney & Schwerner. Do the sweet magnolias blossom round everybody's door? Do folks keep eating possum til they can't eat no more? The ecological balance and the panic for land sends us further North, nobody goes to Alabama even though it's the loveliest place on the continent. Who wants acres of cherries pitted with Coca-Cola post offices and mean penury? Who wants sweet greens and dandelions in January when they are circled round by dusty pickups? Who wants dense forest and sparkling lakes heavy with the theatrical hospitality of the bitter and defeated?

Nobody, that's who, but me. I love the South, and fear it awfully.

If it is the long winter, rocky soil, and short growing season which makes the Vermonter laconic and poor, sure that nothing will work for long, always aware of where those paths of glory lead, then what is it makes the Southerner the same in so many ways? The long summer and dry soil, I guess, but I don't really know. Both characters have little use for the gummint, both have time, both can wait—wait for all this nonsense to stop, wait for you-know-who to rise again, wait for next year, and year after that if I'm not 6 feet under, wait —in truth—for the Whole World to end and be done with it. The suicide rate in Vermont is the highest per capita in the nation, but in the South everybody's dead already. As am I when I pull into Tennessee.

Suffice it to say we slept soundly in Schweid's house in Nashville and I woke with energy and exhilaration to spare at being, again, in the mysterious and challenging land of cotton where I'd surely live if everybody else who lives there would simply move. There, a man knows how to carry his weight with dignity and a lady can be a lay-dee; there, all the fine small things in life are exaggerated and milked to their absolute ends and the mind could roam lazily over every leaf on every tree, returning for a second look, and a thousandth, if you liked, and progress could come to a grinding, sickening halt.

I hate the South like a good boy should, and it certainly wouldn't tolerate me; but . . .

But we rose to good music, Bible and bullshit, on WLAC Radio, where all the commercials are for phonograph records which we'll play for you, folks, in just a minute but listen to this: all the great Bible singers, all the great songs you love to hear again and again, all yours and delivered to your door by the postman for Only Three Dollars; and we ate Supper, for that's what it was, prepared by Schweid's Mother and drove about in a VW Camper provided by Schweid's eloquent Father, and heard the stories of the family and cherished the family mementos; and Nashville was the spot on the map where every mother's son was a guitar-picker and you could pick up the melody on thin air. Michael and I couldn't enjoy it for long, though, as Dale & dug & Schweid could freely do, for we had some unfinished business to tend to down in Alabama, at Selma, we'd promised a beautiful lady to make the scene down there, and a gentleman's honor being only as good as his word, off we went on a 600-mile detour sojourn with parasols and summer in the slow world cresting and winding along the warm Gulf of Mexico, the toastie coast.

The road between Nashville and Selma is one of those unfinished interstate highways which give out on you in the worst places—the city of Birmingham, *par example,*—and whisk you through the lushest, most appealing territory with artificially homogenous landscaping and green signs, green signs by the millions. But Selma is not on that interstate, so we were forced to take the last leg of our trip on a state highway so lonely and so dark in the drizzling, 75-degree night, that we became frightened of all the things not-there, terrified we were of masked marauders behind every hickory, especially since Michael had quite alarmed the teenage watchdogs of the last gas station (their alarm acted out in terms of sniveling are-you-a-girl-or-a-boy humor, twisted smiles) and, having put them thus on the alert, had also informed them of our destination. If they have telephones in Alabama, I said, we may not be so alone as we think; but then we hardly knew what to think anyway, and were dyin' of the heat in our long underwear.

There is a serene quiet, one might almost call it peace, on the streets of an Alabama town once night has fallen; even to us, who live with stillness in winter, the calm and silent night was wondrous beyond words. We got out the parasols, not for effect but because the lady asked us to join her in a stroll, and we paraded the streets at 10 P.M., and met no other wayfarers. "That is the house," she said, "where they filmed that movie, *The Heart is a Lonely Hunter,*" and —as gently and without warning—"Mungo, why do you suppose an old maid in Alabama would go into shock treatments over the death of a young man in Massachusetts?" Why? I had no answer then; but have one now: because the path of true love never did run smooth, because love needs its tombs as well as its living organs, because Alabama is a place to remember, a place where the past does not merely fade into our collective unconscious but is enshrined and revived with each new moon. Sipping tea under that moon could I watch the rest of the world go by, could I dig that universe that does not always pulsate with change, with progress to be unwritten by further jackhammering, but hangs always, like a man lynched, at the same suspended point in time and space.

Six hours of the past proved to be enough for this kid, and when it became time to doze off into the scented beds of Selma, Mike & I rather apologetically boarded Ford Fairlane and beat our bums back over the Tennessee border before the sun could catch us so close to the Gulf, before tropical magnolia evening would give way to the relatively lethargic bustle of Selma by day, and too many unfriendly eyes follow M's ringlets down over his firm Oregonian shoulders. "We now must say goodbye," etc. The superior man is tight & quick, and vanishes before his born enemies can reach for their holsters, and nothing is revealed. Being tight & quick would, in the long run, make us secret bombers of large corporations, as with our brothers who live in New York City and naturally react to it with every sunrise; we are blessed and lucky, we have the right to be loose & fluid most of the time; but in the land of our fathers, in perilous foreign parts in the last week of the last year of the last decade, Tight & Quick was the theme of our movie for we were—you have perhaps noticed—afraid.

The hits just keep on happening.

When I say that we had fear, and imply that the terrorist attacks on the established powers are also a product of fear, I do not mean to exonerate the IBM's and Chase Manhattan Banks of that old world, who deal in fear as their stock-in-trade. I mean neither to condemn those moved to smash and destroy the insurance companies, merchants of fear to Everyman. I mean only that we cannot find hatred in our hearts for men or institutions of which we are not ever afraid, and that our fear is not so much of temporal harm to our bodies—are they coming to take me away? etc.—but of rejection from the human race. Yes what we dread the most is that subhuman treatment, that unspoken or spoken assumption that We are not like Them, that We stand apart, that We are not Their brothers. The unkind word or glance it is, and not the punch in the nose, that kills us. And I mean to leave you with the consideration that it is far easier for this kind of dehumanization to occur in places where many folks live, and we are always strangers, than in other spots where humanity may not so thoroughly cover the face of the planet; and to suggest, as many have before me, that the human survival instinct includes a self-destruct clause applicable to overcrowded situations. And finally: when you can no longer see any real difference between We and They, you've made it to the New Age. I'm not yet there myself.

So Tight & Quick, our movie, was based as much on desire to inflict harm as to escape it in some deep-down real ways, and that has become a whole Outlaw psychology to which any red-blooded dope-smoking kid in my country is at least on occasion victim. The outlaw sons and daughters perform Rip-Offs, in which some unlucky men of means are relieved of one or more of their artifacts, and Burn Schemes, in which somebody or other is hit for money, usually legally. But, as Stevie D. has so well pointed out, no good Burn Scheme is complete until its creator is, himself, Burned. I cannot speak for others who, like myself, propose to write books at a chronological age younger than that at which it is Decent to do so, but this Book and the one before began as Burn Schemes for me, something to make enough money for body & soul to be kept, and of course it is I who is paying the highest price.

We were Tight & Quick, then, because we proposed to have our adventures and live to tell about them; because we did more than once run into dead bodies on the sides of the road, in the newspapers, and in the hearts of our friends; because we looked and felt distinct from the natives of this America, from those who still believe in nationhood & claim to have a nation and a hood of their very own. The black housekeeping lady at the Schweids' house had told us: "You all go down there an' just preten' you're like them, you all talk like them they don' know you ain't just like them. Me, I cun't preten'." But pretending never works, who could we fool if we couldn't fool ourselves?

Nashville, then and again, became our dancehall floor and the band played on through another day and night of WLAC Radio and the great, grave hospitality of Jesus, Mary & Joseph, Doug Kershaw, Bob Dylan, Hello I'm Johnny Cash, 10-year-old spade blues singers, wondrous blind boys by the score, pullulating choirs and fervent soul-savers, hopped-up Chevy road-runners and hominy grits and a thousand dangers without names. But since music supports us more than money or philosophy ever could, and since Nashville's speciality and shuck is music, we were simply happy there, tearing around with Schweid for a guide, ingesting the sacrament in apartments consecrated to rhythm & blues and occupied by struggling pickers out to make their first record contracts, all talented and hopeful in an old-fashioned way that's reassuring in a world so thoroughly fallen-apart as our own. "We need a whole lot more Jesus and a lot less rock n' roll," one song went; and rightly so; for the basic pulse of Nashville is neither existential nor apocalyptic, but easy toe-tapping happiness. Despite these charms, though, our friend Schweid had decided to get on the bus and announced his intention to make a triumphant return to San Francisco with us, making five where three once sat: Michael 'n' Dale 'n' dug 'n' *Schweid* 'n' me now moving West for no reason, braced through Arkansas by a huge sack of sandwiches and fruits packed by S' mother, AM radio blaring Nashville stations clear through to Texas, and approaching the turning of the new year & decade by hours as we nosed toward New Mexico through the ongoing rottenest weather of the century.

Schweid had the look of a pack rat then, emaciated and furry around the edges, like something the cat dragged in; "O, you so *Ogly,*" a frank Southern lady had told him while he was waiting-on in his daddy's store. He has no trace of falseness or tact about him, rather the Neal Cassady of right-now, T & Q to the end, master of the *mot juste;* and this sheer incapacity for ordinary chicanery getting him in trouble at every turn. We met over a woman in 1966, learned to love each other as much as we both did her, I "got" the lady while he hit the road, Schweid the inveterate hetero, beatnik and bum in a time when such things are passé, Schweid the wino and devil and all-night driver and breaker of female hearts; who is my more truthful half; here today, gone tomorrow. The poet who will *never get anywhere,* who has never even had bridges to burn, who can take care of himself—because where he is, help is on the way.

Does it seem to you I am too lavish in praise of my friends, am I hiding their faults and weaknesses from you, can my family be actually so wondrous, noble, talented, and true-blue? Remember these are my friends because they are pillars of virtue to me; because I enjoy their company and hope to learn from them and emulate their ways; because I could not leap joyfully to the side of someone I considered my equal, or less, but only those from whom I can draw new life and inspiration. Increasingly, every body is my potential friend, and I am striving to find the best in each. The bad or weak or petty things are not so important; we all know about such universal human problems, and we are all given over in some degree or other to the devil. But it is the high, honest, and lyric strains in us which are unique and infinitely heartening to every mother's son (are there too many?) crawling with us across the planet.

If there are faults and weaknesses, they are mine, for this is my story after all, and *you* are the friend to whom I now aspire.

Through Arkansas' Ozarks, then, we leapfrogged, singing gaily as we showed our rear to the Mississip, and plummeted into Oklahoma with high hopes of getting through & not noticing the vast sterility of the place, Oklahoma that breaks the camel's back every time. I've never tried living there for a spell, it may be pastoral & idyllic to those content to stay put (the land we belong to is grand): but as a place to suffer through en route to enchanting N. Mex., a place within hollering distance of Asylum yet so many miles long & away, it is insufferable. We lived it all day the last day of what was called Nineteen Sixty-Nine, in short were aware of New Year's Eve, an especially bad time to drive, in an especially icy, unplowed place incompetent to deal with winter-on-the-interstate. Traffic was heavy and moved at a dazzling 15-mile-per-hour pace throughout the afternoon, and the weather (French weather: *temps*) was the most ferocious we had encountered to date; one bad move by a pair of bald Oklahoma summer tires over asphalt slick as glass would kill us, we knew, yet our only defense was to stare harder out the windshield and pray more breathlessly than before for safe deliverance to Texas.

It was in Texas we met Year One. The clock struck 12, the snow had vanished, we had survived the terrible '60's, we were a traveling party of hard-boiled veterans of Youth in Our Time, and congratulated each other and kissed. What nonsense, no, to pay such attentions to an arbitrary calendar, to pretend this night is different from all other nights, when it is simply the same sun and moon and planet going through the same daily routine we hope never to be deprived of? Yes, nonsense, as nonsense has become relief and reason to us, who no longer play the fool for punchclocks or kiss the same asses as have brayed at our fathers these long new decades past. Nonsense, too, because one-half-of-an-hour after 1970 was born, we hurtled over the New Mexico border and discovered ourselves in Mountain Standard Time, that is: back in 1969 by 30 minutes! We hadn't planned it that way, of course, and were temporarily *set back*. But perseverance furthured, as we knew it would, and soon why we jest celebrated & congratulated &.kissed all over again. I thought: would the world were round & wide enough for us to be born into Year One again and again, why stop at only *two* New Year's Eves in an hour's time, why not keep going, keep dying & being reincarnated *all* the Time?

Why not, eh?

Well the fact is *any* excuse for giving yourself a fresh start on life is good enough, whether it be New Year's or spring, your birthday or deathday, it hardly matters; what's important is to preserve the right (for it's yours) to call the past over & irrelevant to the present and future. If we really live with our past, brothers & sisters, we ain't gonna make it. Would you be shocked if I told you it was only a little while before my current body was jolted into Pisces-with-Scorpio-rising that somebody somewhere put six million somebody-elses into gas ovens there to roast & die? Do you think I'd be shocked by the abortion you had when you were 17, your father who buggered you out of junior high, the pills you took while climbing the corporate ladder into thin air? Are we supposed to remember & relive these endless traumas forever? No, no not us because we've got a clean sky above and a fresh sun rising, we've got to start again or none of us shall survive, we're making the Year One a convenient excuse for a new age of reconciliation on the planet, and you're in it whether you thought you were or not because your interest is at stake, you're gonna smile and be happy even if it kills you! No more me? Ah, hah, hah: no more *you!* No more cold!

My old friend Marty had promised that Santa Fe would be 70 degrees in January, that we could work naked in the fields, at least in the afternoons, in unholy defiance as it were of the way things *should & must* be in winter. (You see again how limited my consciousness is —for what do I know of winter in Istanbul or Mexico or the Far East? What do I know of how men treat women there, how youth may roam, how death is feared there?) Alas, for our crowd (which numbers in the billions I'm sure), the seasons will always dictate the mood, at least we are in intimate daily relation with the air and the heavens; and to escape winter is unthinkable, that would be like getting from childhood to man/womanhood without suffering adolescence. Few, if any, societies do not recognize some winter, though the definition of it may vary widely in terms of temperature, precipitation, and duration. Anyway it was *colder* by far in New Mexico than we could remember it being in New England, and those sunwashed fields, deserts really, covered with tough-looking snow, not the kind that invites you to romp & ski, but the other kind that stands in patches and says, "Keep away from me, I'm death itself." Yes, it was bitter cold, dangerously so, when we pulled into defenseless adobe Santa Fe, sitting low to the ground at the foot of magnificent sterile hills on which nothing but the mind may be cultivated. Our friends the Johnsons live some miles out of town, so our tour of Santa Fe by dawn was like a dip on the group roller coaster, we drove through without stopping and headed up into the mountains again with scribbled road directions to an old Canyon.

Just before our road-turnoff, we happened on a gas station and café, which was the first such we'd found in New Mexico, though we drove 6 hours from the border; and the car wanted gas very loudly. Schweid and I in our best road manner, two hardass con guys you better not mess with, who will be terse and gruff and vanish out the door with the coffee in paper cups, entered the café for a snack. But there was a beautiful Indian man, perhaps 50 years old, crinkles in his face and neck and birds-print webs wrinkling from his full eyes; he was dressed contemporary Sears, slacks, sport shirt, some kind of waist-length jacket such as high-school basketball stars wear, seeming to be made of polyethylene. Outasite. He was joking with the waitress, who was clearly also an Indian or *chicano* (Spanish-American to put it badly) and, though middle-aged, lovely in a full way. The man spun around on his stool, and with an easy grin: "Hey, where you cats *from?*" Followed by a laughing, tit-for-tat conversation on San Francisco, New York, New Year's Eve, the weather, etc., at the end of which he insisted on paying for our food. "Hey, look someday

I'll be out on the road and you can buy for me," he said quite soberly. Far-out, we exclaimed, and drove away wondering what great good spirit infuses this place New Mexico, or is it just New Year's Eve, Year One by a few hours? At any rate, it was portentous that the first stranger we met in the year was so trusting, warm, & lively. We fought over mesas and riverbeds dry in most months until we were very lost, seriously worried we could never find the Johnsons' house, when a handwritten note from Marty to me sprang up posted to a tree, and we found our way at last.

The Johnsons, Paul & Becky, came to Santa Fe only a few months before, from New York where they edited WIN magazine and in general kept up. They have three sons, aged ten to fourteen, and are themselves in their early thirties. Paul in particular is remarkably well preserved, and could be taken for a college kid or street hippie with his long blond hair and thick mustache, and it is difficult if not impossible to imagine him as the father of his firstborn son, who is if not a Man at least a peer in every way. They had already retired on a makeshift double bed in the kitchen/common room of a two-room adobe, when our large party arrived. This room, to the point, had the only heat source—a small, drafty fireplace—in the house, which was ill prepared for the bloodless night. The boys had gone to sleep in their own house some hours before. Paul got out of bed and welcomed us in a way that was warm & gentle, so we knew (had never doubted) that no accounting what little these folks had, they would share it with us and it would be, where love is, just enough to go around.

We chatted tiredly and quietly about many things: Indians, climate, compost, horses, dope, friendship, the movement, the quality of life. Until Becky, who had wisely found it unnecessary to stir from her bed, and understood that in our company no tables need be set nor superficial niceties be observed; for we were home; until Becky said Paul, these folks need their sleep more than such talk, there will be time for talk in the morning. And we were taken to the Cold Room, where one bed, a few blankets and sleeping bags, some overcoats and hats and scarves served us regally for sleep. I remember it was cold, crowded, and generally hard on our physical senses, but I also know there was no sense of misery or hard-times, no self-pitying shudder of chill penury, no feeling of anything less than being in a friendly & free place, a place where we would be taken care of: in the style to which we are: accustomed. For the poverty of your hip commune or household is no cousin to the poverty of Holiday Inns and university campuses. There is, often enough, in the psychedelic household, an aura of being in the hands of the Lord, as if anything could happen and we could deal with anything when it comes along.

Sleep now in the desert: Michael 'n' Dale 'n' dug 'n' Schweid 'n' me in a happy lump on the floor, you could not have told one of us from the other 'cause that's the way these kids today *live,* don't ask me just how it happened just take my smiling assurance it's better this way, riskier yes but for higher stakes. Higher and higher. Sleep softly in the broad New Mexico, tall as it is wide, where space surrounds you and the planet holds stubbornly tough and enormous though not even trees can eke much of a living out of it. Sleep soundly under the warm cloak of old friends who shelter you five from the vast sky. Tomorrow Ray and Michael, in their parrying joint-tripmaster roles, will return the car to its owner in Corona, and you need never go anywhere again, need not worry when, if ever, you'll get to California, but take as many days as you need to recover. Take all of Year One if you like, for it will never end you know, last year is always Minus One and next year Plus One. Sleep, then, safe in the cradle of love.

I dreamed my first dream of the West, it goes like this: there is unlimited Kool Space around, and the land is friendly and the atmosphere pleased to enclose you. It is the new, or promised, land and the sunny days over lush beauty have made the local people sunny, too, and the ego may be more free to die. In my dream, I play no part, "I" am scarcely in the dream at all. Michael, alone among us, is a Westerner by birth, and I've been noticing how much faster & brighter his reaction to it is than ours, how he is in tune with this new surrounding while we are just picking up on it in small doses, and so Michael is the star of my dream tonight.

I pay enormous, perhaps unhealthy, attention to my dreams, considering I can't fathom most of them once I'm awake. If I could write this while asleep, we'd both be the wiser for it I'm sure.

On the next day, Paul and Becky's big British van, which blew up every 20 or so miles and was utterly without heat in the 1-below-zero weather, was pressed into reluctant service to accompany us on the 100-mile trip to Corona, so that we'd not be forced to hitchike on back roads in this depopulated state while wind and snow brutally tossed. We made a weird caravan, one swift Boogercar and a ratty old van, as we took the narrow and tilted roads which split the earth like a dagger in those vast high altitudes and nothingness. Corona was infinitely far away, and the car owner a man of unlimited distrust and uptightness, so but for a pretty Mexican waitress in a tiny café and a funny, garrulous Indian who sold us a nonfunctional butane stove (to heat the van and our frostbitten toes) for Ten Dollars, the entire trip was exhausting and lacking many divine aspects. On the way back to Santa Fe, Marty and I huddled under the Irish blanket I'd gotten for Christmas and worn over my knees throughout the journey, Ford heaters notwithstanding, and spoke frankly and warmly though with few words. Marty had left the farm in Vermont some months earlier, disillusioned with the experiment and embittered with some of the people there. It had just stopped working for him, as it must from time to time for all of us, and of course he had to split. We talked, then, for the first time, of many of the farm people, what we felt toward them, what their faults and virtues were; we agreed on most points, more properly: we were in accord, and complemented each other's perceptions rather than competing.

Back at Paul's house, there was the tinest bit of grass, which, once smoked, helped us unravel some basic mysteries by the flickering and smoky fire. The theme ran something like this: why has the population of the darker, more lethargic, warmer continents been for so many centuries smoking cannabis and hashish, eating opium, in general enjoying the psychedelic life, while our own race of white Northern characters have been drinking alcohol and banning the herbs as immoral and illegal? Why, because it was *warm* enough in those darker places to (a) grow the stuff and (b) create little enough necessity for man to labor hard at surviving in that environment. Meanwhile, in fair North America among other places, what grew well was corn, rye, and wheat, grains which fermented produce Liquor, and cold enough to make that false warmness dear and to absolutely necessitate the body & mind be alert for survival. Why then have white Americans suddenly become vastly stoned by the millions? Why, because they have both mastered the transportation problem of all material goods on the planet *and* managed to create an artificially tropical climate year-round in most of their homes: ironically burning up all their storage of natural energy underneath them. Having taken the work out of winter, they have more time for lethargy than in the past, and are more alienated from any individual role in their very own survival!

The Johnsons' house is on the edge of Indian lands, hence protected from urbanization or development in the curious context of Indian-land, land on which treaties and agreements have been systematically and outrageously violated. On these first days of the year, at any rate, the land was surrounded by high hills, spotted here and

95

there with cacti and other desert weed, strong enough to support the family, their dogs, goat, and two horses, but apparently incapable of fertilization by the stinkiest of compost heaps. I was surprised to hear that Paul & family planned to have their garden nonetheless, and easily convinced that they could *make* something grow in it—miracles being, after all, everyday commonplaces these years.

On the third day in Johnsonland, Schweid and Michael and me began to get the spirit for moving on, and elected to bus to Albuquerque—thinking and saying that our removal from the canyon could not but make it more comfortable for the eight people we'd leave behind; and the three of us could no doubt find more physically charitable accommodations in Albuquerque while we were waiting for a new car. We'd take the car, it was decided, back to Santa Fe to pick up dug and Dale and now Marty, who had decided to get on the San Francisco Express, making six in all. (Everybody does everything in groups these days.) Smiling, stuttering Marty led us to some native food which hung tight in my stomach for days afterward, and we boarded the Greyhound to Albuquerque with scores of brown-skinned mamas, knee-booted old gentlemen wearing aviator glasses, Indians wrapped in blankets, the loveliest toughest girls; we rode sixty miles south in a big blue box stuffed with the scattered and multilingual multinational vibrations which have chosen the desert for a home. Were we far-away-from-home or right in it?

In Albuquerque I called Bill Higgs, a Mississippi-born lawyer who works with Reies Lopez Tijerina's revolutionary *chicano* organization, Alianza Federal; could he put us up for a day or two while we got a car and got out? Naturally and of course; and he arrived in dead aunt's inherited Mercury with 14-year-old Orlando, who turned up the AM radio for a song by 10-year-old boy soprano movers & groovers, and I thought well, no more 11 people in an adobe hut, there'll be food & hot water, and we can relax for a while into those middle-class comforts we don't really need but certainly can dig from time to time. But how could Bill Higgs be even remotely middle-class while he was living among a people fighting for land and survival? Bill was living in a two-room adobe heated only by a small potbelly where wood was scarce; his previous house had been firebombed useless by Texas minutemen, and a bomb threat had been lodged against this new house that day; the door to the house fell off its hinges and for lack of a screwdriver could not be fixed; Reies was coming up on trial the following Monday morning and the FBI and CIA apparently heavy underfoot everywhere: so who were we, anglos or gringos, friends or foes, to armed struggling Spanish-American heroes? Could we be trusted? By Bill Higgs of course, but by the *chicanos* why? We had no help to offer them, not even underground newspaper publicity, why were we suddenly tossed in their storm, sharing their scarce food and sleeping under the shadow of their enemies?

Under the Treaty of Guadalupe Hidalgo, much of what I am calling New Mexico belongs to native peoples who've been denied their land without so much as the formality of canceling, altering, or abrogating that treaty. That treaty still stands, but it has been simply ignored. So the brave men & women of the Alianza staged an armed raid on the Tierra Amarilla courthouse in Albuquerque, shot out police cars from machine-gun nests set up on sidewalks, caused the judge to crawl out his window. These guys *really* play rough. Bill took us to the Alianza office, where we were greeted as friends with just the same degree of caution & alienation that Americans can expect from North Vietnamese—we were sympathizers in the struggle, perhaps, but allies hardly. Then he took us to the house under bomb threat, where a small group of teenage boys joked & poked, even flashing a knife or two, playing *Abbey Road* on the Victrola all the while, not scary though, for a poke to these youth is as an embrace between Michael and Schweid and me, their lives are energetic in the use and easy handling of this petty violence.

Still, we sensed being in a place where we did not belong. We went out into Albuquerque-at-large to find the Driveaway Company man (former state policeman, I don't mind telling you boys) who couldn't get a car for us in the visible future. Called the bus company to inquire how many dollars for taking three furry brothers to L.A. or San Francisco? Forty something dollars each, too much. Asked a student at the college there was it easy to hitchhike to San Francisco? Why do it, she said, hitch to Taos instead, *that's* where it's happening! (So who wants to go where it's happening?) With brutal weather, insufficient funds, and angry *chicanos* bracing for the trial of their leader & living as we had been under the barest of shelters, enough already was happening! Went into a bar, where Schweid the barhound sidled up to waitress saying, "Hey, who in this bar can get us to San Francisco? There must be some way out of here!" There, over a dollar pitcher of beer, Michael had his second and I my first *Askeeasko,* and you only get three *Askeeaskos* before you're out!

Askeeasko is what you say when you can't take it any longer— like when somebody gives you a psychic or physical *Peuh.* If a guy walks up to you in Dodge City saloon and *Peuh!* lets you have it right between the eyes, all you can say is *A A A A AskEEEaskO!* You have given up. The other thing you can say, reserved for falling off cliffs & other such absolutely fatal turns of event, is: *Yah-Hoo-Hoo-Hoo-Eee!* But you get only one *Yah-Hoo-Hoo-Hoo-Eee* before you're out.

Went back to the Alianza office, where a meeting was in progress. All the talk was in Spanish of course, so we politely and ignorantly sat through it. An elderly man then inquired of us what was our program? Ahem, well now that you mention it . . . Schweid! What's our program? We told him what we could, how we were trying to be alive in the mother country with neither ecological nor political distortion attached; and he repeated what we said in Spanish to the applause and full cordiality of the audience. The toughest *hombres* of the Southwest said to us: from the podium: you know there is a difference between gringos and anglos, the gringo don't care how much or whether our people are being screwed, maybe a few anglos might *care,* though there is little help they can offer in our fight. So our "program" is no impediment to the *chicano* fight, though it is no solace to them either—and in fact those long-hairs who are doing in New Mexico exactly what we do in Vermont are sworn enemies of the Treaty of Guadalupe Hidalgo merely by their ownership of its territories. It is a foolish notion, this land-ownership; and men are made fools by it. It is a problem for which there is apparently no solution—even those freaks who were, at this time, scheming to buy hundreds of thousands of acres in New Mexico for an absolutely Free Earth Peoples' Park did not seem to realize that it always ends up with the persons living on the land for whom The Land says: *"You* belong to *me."* If you belong to the land, you'll stay there whatever comes, of this I am sure; and if the land belongs to *you,* you'll lose it for sure—perhaps in exchange for dollars, perhaps only in that the exploding, searching, hungry population now vacating the cities will belong to it in spite of you, and insist on it. In short, though the battle for ownership of land seems to be put in legal and financial terms, it is in *emotional* terms that the issue will be resolved: those who must need the land to survive getting it (& it getting *them*) in the wash.

It is precisely because the *chicanos* are owned by New Mexico, in which their culture lies deep and widespread, & because their emotional survival depends on getting it, that I am also certain of their ultimate victory.

In the meantime, there were some desperate & angry *chicanos* in our immediate vicinity and to put it nicely we thought the best move for us would be out of town, and far away from the imminent trial of Tijerina, to which we could offer only three more bodies without reason to be there. Hitchhiking was all we had left for hope, we could neither wait around Albuquerque for a car which might never come, nor return to Santa Fe for our friends; "never look back." And, though we are (as Schweid said quite vehemently) too fucking *old* for hitchhiking in the cold, we asked the kindly Bill Higgs to drive us out to a motel on the edge of town and near Route 66 (Get Your Kicks). "Well, golly, I hope you guys are gonna be all right," Bill said as he left us with the proprietors of the Apache Lodge, 4 dollars a night & 50 cents extra for TV. He is bold and courageous, walks on crutches, lives in a doomed house, has a cause in which he is both involved & accepted: and hopes *we* are gonna be all right! "Bill," sez I, "don't worry about us. We are in the hands of the Lord." "Have been," he returns, "for a long time."

After two days and nights in Albuquerque, then, we are sitting out dawn in a locked motel room packing our lives as tightly & quickly as we can fit them in canvas bags and cardboard suitcase—on which I have written CALIF in brown masking tape. The next stop, San Francisco, seemed to my incredulous eyes over the Standard Oil map some 1,200 miles away! Michael in his fashion turned to the *I Ching* instead and got the hexagram "Treading the Tail of the Tiger, Yet It Does Not Bite the Man." You are on a most perilous hairy-scary journey, the good book said, and death & danger surround you, but you will emerge unhurt y'know why? Because this journey is undertaken in the spirit of good fellowship & good cheer! Decorum brings success, it said, and even irritable people can be handled by pleasant manners. We were reassured by the warm, wise abstractions the *Ching* offered, juxtaposed as they were with the grim realities of bitter winter and the Apache Lodge.

Next morning, we walked six long tall miles to the freeway entrance, turning and resting every ten or fifteen minutes and watching, by degrees, the city of Albuquerque in which we'd been small, grasping life, become a tiny burg nestled under a towering white mount and 360-degree blue sky. How good, how good to be leaving the tight and troubled city behind us again, and heading out into the hills: despite the cold and the risk of being stranded, getting arrested even. We waited perhaps two hours for our first ride, a cleancut Adonis and his fair lady, he from Oregon, she from Vermont, now teaching Navajos in a village 50 miles off the highway from Thoreau, New Mexico. I imagined they were salaried by VISTA or some liberal church, for they were the sort of beautiful young couple who could con a well-heeled sponsor like a pushover; but they were gentle & kind to us, picked us up after all whereas many hundreds of autos, some bearing furry brothers who'd wave and sign us with a V, had passed us by.

So it was in Thoreau that we had to find our next ride, in the heart of the desert, and it was in Thoreau we whiled away the day and into the night, getting progressively colder and more hungry, sure after thousands of refusals that no stranger would risk our company this night, and we'd die in Thoreau, too. Schweid became slightly hysterical, began to dance & perform other histrionics designed to excite the pity of the fat comfortable many who stank and roared and wheezed past us in that forbidden untamed Thoreau. I realized we *could* die, one or more of us could lie flat and stiff on that snowfield over there, and it'd merely *decrease* our chances of getting a ride. For those who passed us by, even longhairs in empty VW buses with Ohio plates, the world was warm and fast, like a portable livingroom; they did not feel the wind, they did not hear our stomachs rumbling, they could not even relate to us, who were outside and alive while they had become vestigial parts of their operating autos. And Michael it was who discovered that the ever-present V sign, flashed from behind the plastic driving wheel by somebody who won't even slow down for dying folks on the roadside, that V sign doesn't mean "Hi" or "Me too"—it means what the upraised middle-finger used to mean!

Dark fell and we gave up. Die, die then, o my soul, die with Thoreau who lived by it! Fall by the wayside where the whole of the world is speeding past unmoved! Things had, decidedly, gotten out of hand.

But a small, new BMW stopped shrieking over our bier, and a mewing Siamese kitten jumped out. I tried to talk sense to the cat, but only Josh who'd been driving with neither sleep nor pills since Philadelphia, could persuade it, in Italian, to get back in the car. A joint or two was then unwrapped from Josh's matchbox stash, the heater turned up, and off we went to: San Francisco! Josh, it developed over the many miles, was a scholarship athlete at Stanford University whose natural and seemingly unlimited energy came of Scorpio-Scorpio-Rising; his daddy had been an Alaskan explorer so he was raised up there in the long nights; he smoked no tobacco, saving his lungs for that good California grass, and with his life he proposed to make movies! He was 20 years old. He stood in awe of our worldly ways, our talk of farmin' and truckin' and writin' books for fancy New York publishers; and we in awe of his very mortal frame. It was companionship conducive to high times, though, and we lightly floated all the way to California without much real misery. Once in the Bay Area, we knew, we'd be taken care of, we could go comfortably mad, and stay stoned *all* the time, and live off the fat of the land.

Pulling into San Francisco, now, from the East and North, Michael and Schweid were hoppin' up and down in the back seat, going Whooee! We Gonna Have Some Fun! and Josh, ever-calm but strong, smiling broadly behind the wheel, thinking of times past and future, his studies, and some little lady no doubt. Only me was freaking and didn't know just why. Only me was saying, at first to myself then aloud, NO NO, Turn Back! as the lights of town came closer and brighter and the green signs read "Fell Street" and "Civic Center" and the painted billboards said Slip Into Something Comfortable (big booger jet), Go to New York! What's *wrong,* man? Well it's just that . . . it's *evil,* man, it's the wrong place, O I will be silent now and not bum your trip. But as street lights & traffic & the infamous vertical hills & row houses all came into view, and the smell of petulia oil (they say it's an aphrodisiac) floated heavily on the street & in the air, and as somebody was going out for the homecoming lid or four of really dynamite stuff, as all this was happening: I slept on a nearby tousled mattress, insisted on going to the bus station, and left town mere hours after having arrived from 14 days trip—without even thinking twice.

II. My Second Dream of the West

O, I returned to San Francisco of course, as we all must, but not before blue Pacific, tall Redwoods, Mendocino: and the life within home and hearth, you might call it West Coast Commune Scene, had played itself out. The apartment to which Schweid had taken us in the city had a small hand-lettered wooden sign in its chaotic decadent living room: saying only *Mendocino*. It might have once been used as a hitchhiking sign for somebody going north from San Francisco but it had ended up on the chipped and tired mantel, which covered a fireplace useless now but for a gas space heater. I remembered vividly: a similar apartment in Cambridge, Massachusetts, which boasted for decoration a wooden sign *Vermont,* a sign which I myself had used on the road north from Boston.

Had I come through hell and cold, through darkest Pennsylvania, bebop Nashville, tepid Alabam, through treacherous Oklahoma and uncomfortable New Mexico, Arizona, California, to arrive at the same place I had left? Was not San Francisco just like Cambridge? Then the wooden sign told me what I had to do: Mendocino!

Mendocino sits very dangerously on the rocky rainy coast, rising up from the ocean into cliffs & high woods the sheer wonder of which had stoned many a head before mine. Many artists came to see it, to re-create it. It must have seemed to an earlier generation the most awesome spot on the globe; and those who could afford it "bought" Mendocino, tucked their little homes & studios into its impossible curves and crannies and settled down. The friends I had come to see, whom I did not know before I got there, were artists, too, but in the absolute sense of my age-group: in which everybody (it seems) is an artist, one and all re-create life and we never ask each other "what do you *do?*" in the sense of "how do you make money?" Many of us make no money at all, others do but it is something less than incidental to our lives, which are really about a million forces having nothing to do with career, profession, or money; we fish, farm, draw, paint, write, love, drive about in cars, cook, bake, give birth, redecorate, build, destroy, you name it; and reserve the right to stop whatever we're doing and do something else, just for the hell of it.

The only possible approach to Mendocino is on old Route 1, the famous scenic route which distinguishes California road-builders as men who at one time had more vision for dream and fantasy than for practical things. Route 1 is barely passable now, washed out in parts from the heavy winter rains, and perilous beyond all reasonable expectations; in short, it conforms to the demands of the sea. "The town has no need to be nervous." The ocean pounds at Mendocino's front door, the Bank of America branch office, and small lean-to Main Street with two groceries and a gas station and one old hotel. The whole thing feels ready to sink. (Tie up the boat in Idaho?) I'd been dreaming all across the continent of, silly, a red VW Squareback station wagon: like this particular car was coming to get me and it'd be great when it happened. Sure enough then, the very vehicle appeared before me in the pounding night, my old friend Paul of the long blond California hair (though himself a Massachusetts boy like me, they become California kids after six months, for who is a native in those parts, and what difference would it make anyway?) and a lady of ravenlike dark hair named Miss Lark with small child Little Aeko, at the wheel. Off, then, into the enchanted red forest where a man can still get a square meal and the skies are not cloudy all day.

I took up living in a polyethylene house built atop a dead Rambler, proof to my astounded eyes that both cars and plastic were good for something when the ingenuity of free men is given rein. The house was utterly clear on both walls and roof so I had the sense of living in the outdoors, which was never colder than 50 degrees F. and always wet. A small Aladdin heater kept the dampness out and I was happy, as they used to say, as a pyg in shit. The folks who lived in that place were what Verandah and I would have called *first-class freaks* only a few years ago, and they had of course the best of everything: water fit to drink, air easy to breathe, natural piety, whole grains for munchies, fresh-caught abalone, warm bread with butter and a certain unreluctant pursuit of the truth. *"It's all the same,"* I exclaimed. Michael's no fool, and within a day or so he showed up in Mendocino too.

Busy busy busy the group mind was going through some heavy changes, everybody was giving it away; Paul gave me a blank check with his signature on it, which I took to the Bank of America and cashed for 9 dollars: for a man with good boots on his feet and 9 dollars in his pocket can get most anything he needs in this world. Lark gave me the promise of paradise, but like a fool I failed to collect. Alan pounded his day's catch of abalone Bang! Bang! (they tighten their muscles when caught, so you gotta beat 'em soft) and gave me to eat with a broad smile and stories of ages ago in Berkeley Movement Days. Jeez, I coulda stayed at that place forever y'know and got treated like a king: among gods. The ocean alone served to remind us of our stinking mortality, saying *Mendocino, and all who*

trip and tarry there; Mendocino, Mendocino, I'll get you in the end.
"And in the end, the love you take is equal to the love you make."

Paul & Carolanne were readying for a big move to an island off British Columbia, accessible only by water and of course in a foreign country; is that the next step, I wondered? Paul did a whole number on my head of how even fabulous Mendocino and glorious Vermont are not good enough for us anymore, no a new generation of city dropouts is coming along and it is for them that Mendocino remains; for us, who flatter ourselves with the notion that we are always a coupla years ahead of the real stampedes (*viz.,* antiwar movement, dope, rural relocation), for us there must be higher and further-out places: B.C., Ireland, Greenland, whatever. We see the issue, the problem, of overpopulation plain in its face: and we run to wherever there is the most room and the toughest conditions, wherever we can most easily adjust without distorting the ecological balance. Mendocino and Vermont now have an overpopulation problem, too: not akin to the likes of San Francisco or Boston to be sure: but growing fast. *The marathon goes on and on and on; how long can they last?* [1] Where will we go when there is nowhere to go?

Go north, now, out of Mendocino and into the giant Redwoods who say nothing & know it all; Ronald Reagan says of Redwoods: "You seen one Redwood, you seen them all." I say Right On, Ronald!; the only problem being if you see one, you see none at all, for they too travel in groups you know, and their soul rises proud and tall in vast forests where they seem to hold the earth, and our minds, together. Gaston St.-Rouet, last seen marching in the anti-inaugural parade in Washington, D.C., accompanied me through the big woods with nothing less than the cosmos now on his mind; playing his flute to the mammoth stalks our mother, and I holding fast with both feet planted in the ground, craning my neck upward and upward, crying for joy at

[1] From a movie: *They Shoot Horses, Don't They?*

the exhilarating rush of energy from their ancient supply. There is only one place on the map where redwoods deign to grow, and that is reason enough if you need one for California to be called holy. And, as I am no priest, how could I make the trees real to you, how sing their praises in any hymn which could not be desecration and blasphemy? In this context, nothing is revealed.

When we emerged from the magnificent forest, as from church, dazzled and energized by our big OD of living godhood, it was to more roaring and wheezing of internal-combustion engines, this time long trucks carrying dead redwoods to the cemetery, chained together and stacked in pyramids like corpses after the Plague; like common peasants, these princes were being sliced down and shipped off to some cheap and razzle-dazzle end. Redwood tables for deathly restaurants? Redwood pendants from the yard-arm end, like the eardrop I gave to Haight-Ashbury Molly? "Nice" house (read morgue) for up and coming exec in Palo Alto? How, then, shall we worship to a McCullough Chain Saw after the Redwood Lord thy God; thou shalt not have false gods before thee.

Put it bluntly raymond: save the redwoods, let us together, or die like dogs!

Like dogs shot in Vermont woods for running down deer some person wants to shoot next October for the sport.

Further north, further north, until our minds are off these morbid affairs, until mountains run high capped with white flowers and the earth is whole.

Following the old roads, the scenic highways, which dip and splash quite nearly into the ocean and are bumpered on the east by the great trees which never let us down; with Gaston in his '53 Chevy who will not exceed 40 mph though she couldn't, under the weather anyway; 300, 400, 500 miles from San Francisco: on to Oregon! Grant's Pass and a town called Tekilmah where every house is a commune and we can sip tea playing mouth-harp and listening to the never-ending rain.

We'd picked up some hitchhikers who took us to their communal house. It rains in Oregon as in few other places, day and night for months at a time, and the rain throws a shroud over the green universe there, as if Oregon is lush and beautiful and would be an incomparable playground 12 months of the year if only that wetness would lift. The rain is called Winter, because it keeps us indoors as much, perhaps more, as the snow & cold do in other places—how odd to find such a green-grass and full-tree world forbidding and dangerous. But the home folks in Tekilmah were so glad to have their lost ones back that they shrugged off what had clearly been a deep depression at their inability to get a fire going; all the wood was wet. And, like Alice and her animal friends, who danced to get dry, we made music to get warm. It worked like a charm.

Skinny Gaston, whose long hair made his nearsightedness all the more difficult to work around, and whose auto was like a parody of hippie-cars, bashed and bruised and incapable of "passing inspection" (an Eastern assumption, this compulsory biannual scrutiny of cars, which is nothing less than a racket managed by the garages and the State), lived on a level from which I could learn much: slow down, slow down, was his major advice. We took two days to travel from S. F. to Michael's home town of Salem, Oregon, and it took me some eight or nine days to get out of there once I got into the rhythm of the place. We took day-trips to the furious and unrelenting coast, and watched it pound fruitlessly on the rock surface of the land's edge, similar to Maine if you've ever been there, and no cousin to the loose sands on which California is built. Gaston stood on Michael's Mother's lawn playing his pipes to her astonished ear and tickled ribs, and though inflation had struck home and this great and good lady was having some troubles with her checkbook (as such problems have now become familiar to every American home, and subject matter no doubt for old-fashioned cartoonists of the domestic scene), she was lavish and full in her hospitality and we rested comfortably in the lap of suburbia until we could no longer bear it, and security seemed too literally around the corner.

Mr. Somebody-or-Other says "now's the time to buy." But there's nothing valuable or desirable for *sale* anymore.

Michael's friend Jimmy, who shaves his head every Vernal Equinox, knew a cabin in the sopping forest of Oregon where we could go; it was North, of course, so we went. I made oatmeal or popcorn or one of those easy things, and we sat by the crackling Franklin stove luxuriating in the lack of electricity and the stillness of the night. This boy, Jimmy, was a righteous religious fellow, and so fearless and forthright in his declamations on the quality of life on the planet, so obviously a member of our family, that I set out to convince him to come home with us, and without much effort did just so. We'd bring Jimmy home, I thought, like a souvenir, and he'd help us (as he helps himself) get straightened out. He is both a lover and student of the occult—not only in books but in his inner-mosties—and a quick and deadly accurate judge of character. ("Raymond Mungo, I'm going to beat you on the head with this stick if you don't *shut up!*") When it's time you had somebody look you straight in the eye and tell you what in you is just unbearable, I hope you may find as compassionate a shrink as our Jimmy under *your* bed.

We are our own shrinks, you know, because we see each other all the time and know the score, and at the same time are independent of each other, genetically and financially: nobody keeps anybody in any communal household, each of us could, and probably will, split on a moment's notice. To return again another day. And it sure beats 50:dollar sessions with bearded weirdos in air-conditioned anterooms.

We went 800, 900, 1000 miles from San Francisco, by thumb and Trailways, till we ended up in Seattle, Washington, where the rain stopped for the first time in the three weeks I'd be on the lam on the W. C. Seattle is where the Japanese Current strikes home and sweet grandmothers living in houseboats offer you tea, cookies, or Mexican marijuana. (We had some of each.) I'd often wondered how long it would take and what it would be like when it came to really *old* people smoking dope—as really young people are now doing, I'm told. Based on our experience in Seattle and elsewhere on the W. C.—for it seemed, all at once, we were running into 50-year-old lady doctors and respectable small-town professionals aged 60 or more who were wrecked out of their minds—my impression is that the older they smoke, the groovier they are. Even if we had wanted to blow that houseboat grandma's mind, I doubt we could have succeeded—she was so thoroughly blowing *ours* with her stories of life around, husbands, children, jobs, places, and of course her dynamite stash. She seemed ready to *take off* at any unforeseen moment, and we walked her plank laughing easily at the wonders that never ceased around here.

Well, you can't blow minds of course until your own mind is blown, and though she was born a long long time ago, your mother *should,* damn it, know!

In Seattle, too, we found the elusive Driveaway Man and picked up a new Dodge Corona Deathtrap machine bound for Washington, D. C., the nation's capital—that was the best we could do, I swear —and drove it down to San Francisco with the idea of picking up those we'd left behind, and anybody else in the mood for going, for the return trip East. In view of the rain, which began again only a few miles south of Seattle, Michael elected to take the interstate freeway, which was faster and more inland, hence less liable to be flooded than the coast routes. When we got roughly parallel to Mendocino, he figured, we'd find a cross route and go there to spend the night.

It was on this long trip through the Northwest wilderness that I had my second dream of the West.

It had been raining in Oregon and California for some 30 days with only occasional respites, and for I think 17 days and nights without stopping at all in northern California. This kind of weather, I was told, is worse than normal. At any rate, the land of sunshine and plenty seemed to me a world of incessant downpour and mudpie spirits for the entire month of January, and I thought I'd best go away since it was bringing me no relief and who knows maybe if I leave the sun'll come back. Certainly, most of the old friends I'd managed to locate in the Bay Area were not up to psychic par— almost as if the mood of the East had been strangely transferred to the West on airwaves. The dream began, thus, in a California merely grey and chilly and less than inspiring.

It quickly turned to a nightmare. In brief, the land began to give out, the inland freeway was clotted with landslides and huge rocks, traffic had been rerouted to one-lane, and in part the freeway itself was actually under inches of water. If we needed some colossal bummer at home to get us moving toward California, then surely it would take an even bigger sadness to make us leave it once there; and this was it. The Dodge inched perilously past countless places where the sides of hills had caved in, past houses sliding helplessly into ravines, charging through small lakes in the road, skidding and floating on them, and still the rain came whipping down. There is probably nothing more frightening on the material plane than the earth itself moving under you, and we were terrified: odd, you see, because I often feel unafraid of mortal death: but death in California, by landslide, O it would have been too, too banal and undignified! A crackling voice on the AM radio kept interrupting the steady diet of Year One pop music ("Smile On Your Brother," "He Ain't Heavy, He's My Brother," "Walk a Mile in My Shoes," you know the scene) with hysterical reports of whole neighborhoods which just disappeared under the weight of the storm. And we had all read *Esquire* and knew of the infamous San Andreas Fault, and moreover knew that we were sitting on it!

I dreamed, not that California was falling into the ocean, but that the ocean was coming up to eat California. Cruel fate! Those who had hoped to be destroyed by a romantic, thundering earthquake would instead be slowly engulfed by an ordinary, if unending, shower! Crueler still: that we who wanted nothing more than a safe place to be crazy for a while should go down with the ship, indistinguishable from the permanently crazed ones who had settled down into it!

We made it to Mendocino lonely in our Corona, stopping once to remove a large tree which had become uprooted and fell across the highway, otherwise just dodging landslides, puddles, and falling rocks. It was a miracle we got there, naturally, but we wanted a Last Look at the blue Pacific before it became too brown and muddy with the sunken civilization of California. We accepted some abalone shells from Alan as bye-bye gifts, and went down to the beach. Walking up from the water's edge to where we had parked the car, we had a very hard time of it as the land beneath us caved in, slid over, and nothing would do for support. Roots and vines and big boulders sank under my weight (113) and went tumbling into the sea. Michael was now the most frenetic of the three of us, and insisted on getting to San Francisco, picking up our friends, and getting out of there without so much as a parting joint. And that's what we did.

By the time that car really stopped, we were in Utah, heading into the Rockies, looking for the highest spot on the planet accessible to an automobile. Dale, dug, and Schweid in the backseat were shaking off their sleepy San Francisco apartment-scene heads (it gets to you very fast); Michael, Jimmy, and me in the frontseat wishing we could fall into hushed peaceful slumber.

III. ideath

From these strong hills, in late winter, safe from the perils of the wild West and ready to hibernate, we now leaped wide-eyed and alert in the middle of the night; there now came a tremor in the earth which was new to us.

The late winter, more than any other season, locks us in and ensures our privacy, mud season in March forbids autos within miles of our cottage, bitter winds and the accumulated snows of yesterday make the universe outside forbidding and dreary, wood supplies run low and wet till we huddle all in one over the same stove, foodstuffs preserved and frozen from summer run out altogether, automobiles die clanking and unregistered, all the money's gone, we burst into a full year's close saving of tears.

All that was enough for us a year or two gone, but this late winter holds in store something more terrible by far, and more miraculous. We die.

We always knew it would happen this way, we couldn't have foretold just when, we put it off while there was any straw to cling to, but now it's take-your-medicine-month and face the music: we die.

It starts with crying and shaking all over and kneeling to god Ashley for comfort which it cannot give; it continues into distrust of words and incomprehension of their meanings and wondering if any person any place could understand; it goes on into helpless surrender before the demons of darkness and the waves which vibrate around our heads; it ends with a kiss. We die.

The words have built up over the many years until they strangle us. Raymond chokes and gags on his own words: where is the fool who allowed such words to accumulate so, what of those who have been listening and suffering the unending flow of words from his foul mouth, why is there so little wisdom and so much pride in those words? See Raymond wildly stuffing his back pages, correspondence, manuscripts into the Ashley and warming chill bones over their fire. For a moment's quiet warmth, were they worth all the arrogance and temporal braying? Raymond, the anal-retentive filing-cabinet mentality, is at last forced to chop off his head in order to clear his throat.

The seed has built up unspent until it burns us out. The sap has been tapped into buckets—books, poetry, bread, carpentry, academe, pen-and-ink, post-offices, autos, hospitals, cows, roads, gardens— until it no longer reached the limbs of the tree. The tree was dead and fit for chopping and burning in the long night. But hold: see patience and healing and grafting and fucking try, slowly but surely, to make it Bloom again. See touching and reaching and hugging and kissing and five long bodies all evening on the floor in a quivering wondering mass. See Wrongness and Weirdness and Mustn't and Shame crumble in the face of the emergency at hand. Stamp out Couples! Admit it, propose it, then do it! See four or four million new angels burst blindly to life in the rattling loins of the ladies around: great promise for the harvest moon! No marriage, no papers, no owners of life yet unborn! Come fall there'll be wailing of mothers and babies who'll choose for themselves from a galaxy of fathers, each one in his way Responsible. We die and rise the same.

The tears have built up untumbling until they drown us. Each is a reservoir wide and deep as the miles we have tripped on the planet. We go under. Fighting for air in our Davy Jones' lockers, like whalers of old we are trapped in the belly; with salt in our eyes and on our tails and all over our stinging bodies, where shall we find the sea vast enough to take what we have to get rid of? We are kicking and pounding the earth of our backbones, trying to make rivers run where the roads behind us are caked and dried by the sun. Nothing works.

Priests come to anoint us and whisper their vespers over identities now obviously finished. Poor Michael, he was a nice enough chap, we knew him well. Dan comes in white denims from Mill Valley, where Blue Cheer grows on the trees, speaks softly, and moves silently from room to room, like a mother protective of charges. (We have no mother to suck off.) Paul comes from Mendocino, speaks loudly and brightly, declaims o'er our bodies like an orator fresh out of Yale; "and *this* one, will she come back a Woman who was only a Cook?" Luis comes from Cuba and Cambridge, enormous and jolly, with gifts for the family to lessen their grief: Mamoushka and Bubbles, a dog and a bus. Susan comes from New York, all lovely and innocent, she is a stranger who sees what is happening and at once understands; she will take care of her end of the bargain, arrange for the funeral and send out the cards. Steve, Janet, and David all come as a group: to whip up hot chocolate and serve it in cups, sew pockets, read stories, and generally make the time fly.

What's happening here is happening everywhere, they come from all over to see if it's true. Even the dogs know something is up, they vanish together to leave us alone, we can't count on *them* as objects of love any more.

It is moving so fast. Where is it going? What does it matter? Are *you* still with us? Will there really be Spring?

Peter can't wait. He challenges Michael to wrestle him down in the barn. An enormous crowd gathers to whistle them on and wonder if it's for real. Can a pacifist wrestle? I'm thinking when *Peuh!* there's a struggle and devils are flying clear up through the rafters, the hayloft is shaking with honest hostility, my god this could get out of hand! But Michael can't see with his hair in his eyes, so he cuts it all off! Bridges are burning. We can see by his cheekbones he's only a boy, maybe even a baby, he's got a fresh start. Get out the scissors!

See Verandah and Raymond, Jimmy and Richard, Johnny and Steve, get their hair cut. Don't worry kids, they say it keeps growing even after you're dead. There's enough hair in this family to make a fur coat! We won't need one. The neighbors are dazzled, can it be it was only a passing fad after all? We look in the mirror, we cannot believe what we see: us. You. Children again, but all different. And it isn't even Spring.

But don't stop there, with the hair. Don't stop. It's always Year One.

We were climbing the mountain after gathering the mail (they refused to deliver from November to May), no sap was yet flowing and winter still doing her worst. "O, Michael," said Raymond, "I see by the paper" (which he'd culled from the postbox) "that 400 orphans were ravaged by buggery on a backstreet in Tangiers. Moreover, a judge in Chicago sent three nuns and five poets to jail for their lifetimes for farting out of turn. And they're putting an interstate right through our outhouse!" *"That's just what I mean,"* he returned. "O, Connie," said Bob, "did you see by the Times that they're tearing down Luxembourg to make a new airstrip for Paris? And taxes are up in Brazil? And a young man was crucified, just for the hell of it, by reckless collegiate associates down in the South?" *"No I hadn't,"* she sighed. "O my god," cried Verandah, "I read in The Globe how starvation and war, drug addiction and pestilence have now been repackaged in a movie which opened to raves in New York. And you mustn't eat Portuguese caviar, it's said to have worms." We looked at each other hard and fast: we'd quit our TV and given up telephones, eat CaCa food only when desperate, were phasing out cars and electricity: why read the papers?

We canceled the papers. At first it was hard, our last link with bad news, now how would we know where misery had latest struck? But then it got easier, and finally blissful, we still know of war & famine & plague, we're learning why these things are so, and why they will not, in the future, be. But we don't need that tidy and O-so-efficient daily compendium (gathered for somebody's profit and everyone's bummer) of all the worst tidbits of suffering in last 24 hours. That's no way to be born!

There was always the mail, but it stopped. On strike. O they kept on delivering circulars, junk, such things of which you could always start fires—but letters from friends, nevermore. It is clearer and clearer, is it not? There is some vast conspiracy to wipe out the past, to give us that clean slate we long for; alienated no more, we must carry our messages right on the beam, appear there in person to bring the good news, or don't bring any.

Don't stop there. Don't stop there. Spring is coming.

There is music. When we play to funerals, we play the march from Saul. Hear the dead winter night, when nothing stirs, broken by black music, soul music, guitar, accordion, piano, mouth-harp, cymbals and drums; mantras, chants, rhythms for maple-sugaring, climbing hills, building fires. See the magic band of crystal-clear heads playing, singing, wailing, to levitate the tractor from where it has been sunken in ice since November! See the tall black magician, Taj, pick banjo all the livelong evening just like on the records, but realer & truer; we kidnapped him. Where is the body that need not move and groove with the tempo? Lullaby the sun to sleep, sing it up again in the morning; howl at the moon. "And the seventh brings return; darkness increased by one." If we sing and play truly, and give rise to every note in newborn souls, can we fail to bring the spring?

We are indistinguishable from spring, nothing will stop us now, it grows closer, it grows closer, we will make it happen and anything else to happen which we please: thunder and rain, electric storms, shooting stars, crimson heavens, endless sun, we are unpredictable and primitive, we are bigger than us, just keep an open mind.

Just wait and see, we will make green grass grow, peaches blossom, flies drop eggs and multiply, water gush and sparkle, corn soar toward paradise, mountains lurch from their resting-places, sunsets undulate and quiver. We are tubes through which all life blows.

And yet we are dead—strangled, burned, drowned, frozen. In hiding under the crusted Earth, though, something more wonderful than our death was terrifying: and more impossible to describe. We are not authors of books, farmers, or freaks any more; we are life waiting to burst wildly and beyond control into nobody's vision, not even our own. We know nothing yet, we are nothing yet, compared to what we shall be. Nothing is our language, music is our medium, spring is our cue to go right on. We are in the eye of the storm, and it's coming your way.

Pay attention to the eye. Don't look at the hair, cause the hair is neither here nor there. Don't listen to the words, cause the words can only cloud the truth. Don't look for the clothes, cause the clothes are beside the man and it's all the same beneath them. Pay attention to the eye: look straight in the eye: cause the eye don't lie.

The I lies deep in fallow ground now, it took care of itself. We are waiting for spring. We are waiting for spring. It will not be long. For whatever sleep remains now, in the stillness of the aftermath, good night.

—March 1970

Peeling off the Layers

Waffled-white,
and intricate as underwear,
we wore the winter
like a pelt,
until the thick of it
became our skins.
The touch of it had nerves enough.

Huddled at the stove,
all still as a circle of gargoyles,
muffled to the fingertips
in counterpane, our
coat of arms,
the nails remained exposed
like claws
to turn a page,
or itch among the inches
of our clothes.

What is warm?
The firelight barely reignites
a memory.

The menfolk snore like polarbears.
The women, brittle as stalactytes
dream like schoolmarms:

* * *

When your love had turned to water
(cold to hold,
yet tangible as a fistful of ice, it was),
spilled through the cracked cup
of my palms,

I turned aside my finery,
rolled down remembering
as ladies in a world at war
remove silk stockings,
thin as membrane,
precious as the notion
of love not rent
from thigh to toe.

Reclining in the bath,
where gravity is less than earth,
a lady, soap-fleeced,
shorn of stockings,
might admire,
as if it were a mannequin's,
the end
of what was once
a well turned ankle . . .

* * *

The sun ignites one morning
like a furnace in the eastern sky.
We sever us from sleep

and one by one assemble
in the yard
for peeling off the layers of wool and gloom
to flesh,
Our shy bones crack like knuckles
in the heat,
our muscles twitch like frogs' eyes.

The soil revealed beneath the flood
(snow, grey & weary as a union suit
in May),
is bristled, stubbled, soft
and clammy with matted grass,
as winter legs,
our walking sticks.

—Verandah Porche

3. WARM:
Total Loss Farm

for Steve Diamond, the King of Hearts

Of all delectable islands, the Neverland is the snuggest and most compact; not large and sprawly, you know, with tedious distances between one adventure and another, but nicely crammed. When you play at it by day with the chairs and table-cloth, it is not in the least alarming, but in the two minutes before you go to sleep it becomes very nearly real. That is why there are night-lights.

—J. M. Barrie, *Peter Pan,* 1911

Where does the gone sanyashin live? The gone old man of cold mountain? Where does any He/She that's gone beyond live? Why on Total Loss Farm, of course. On no other earth can we plow, nowhere else does the tree of goodloving grow.

—Luis Yglesias, in a letter

The pearl is only the oysters' autobiography.

—Federico Fellini

Let us begin at the old apple tree. "Turn right at the old apple tree," the directions read plain as day, and then "straight on till morning." You can remember, because you relive it, and relate to it fast as the sun. Without it, we'd never get home.

Once it bore fruit. An impossible temptress it must have been, luring small boys and young lovers with meaty red spheres cast against a sea of green—for it stands alone, arms outstretched to merciless heavens, twisted and gnarled, delicious as sin. Now it is only a marker for travelers, but none can resist it and each stops on his way to admire what it has been. It has weathered all storms, so it stands intact, and an evil wind indeed it would be that blew it down. And though it has no more children, yet it buds and blossoms with tiny green leaves in the spring.

You can remember. You can remember. How it was the first time you saw it, not a tree merely but a monument to the goodness of time and the greatness of God. You first saw it in spring but by summer you'd climbed it and got yourself sticky with its running bark, and grinned from the top branch with the knowledge you were higher even than the barn—higher than anything but birds. So it is always with children and trees. It is really that simple. I have often heard adults say "Going forward is difficult, going backward is impossible," and perhaps it is true, then why grow up at all? Slow down. There are fruits and berries, fishes and game, trees and bushes and pine groves and people with faraway looks in their eyes in the place we are going. Everything comes to he who waits, lives, and dies with the mystery, but it's ever so easy to miss it entirely if we take it too fast. Some might even imagine it's an ordinary farm (something I've never encountered), or even a temper of the times, a college or church or weird reservation. We won't make those mistakes, will we? We've sailed the wild Conc and Merry, bumped across the great divide, even died in the process, now it's time to stay home for a spell.

The apple tree is our sentry, she guards our surprises from view. Beyond her, a road made of earth (not dirt, for there's not so much as a gravel and nobody keeps it in shape) bends sharply to the right and steeply uphill toward . . . what? Can't tell yet. The road goes for two miles before we are there, the children call it the longest driveway in town. At its end is the farm. I'll cheat a little and give you some clues: it's not in "Vermont" or anywhere else with a name and a tax-rate. It's not on any chart, you must find it with your heart, Mary Martin said that. It's a myth and I'm fooling you, or maybe just fooling myself. It's called Total Loss Farm because it produces nothing visible to the mature eye—all the livestock, machinery, seeds, and such tools and not even one peach or can of maple syrup makes it as far as the market. And nobody who goes in there to stay has ever been seen alive again.

Total Loss Farm: *lose yourself.*

* * *

Beyond the apple tree and over the crest in the road, we might see a million things. This could be a tropical detective story, with palm trees and shutters and fans on the ceiling that lazily turn and never really get anywhere. The trees might bear mangoes, papaya, bananas, as likely as cherries or pears. A moment from now, it's wild Colorado, Montana, the High Sierras; water as clear as the firmaments rushing through tall forest glades, and anybody you meet will be ruddy and wholesome. Then it's suddenly arctic Siberia, an island, a desert, a mountain. All that it's not, all that it's never, is the city, it can't be mistaken for that. It's too wild, too beautiful; and even if it's bleak and depressing, and our friends at the top of the hill uncordial and surly, we'd still know it was good, honest, and uncompromising —there is little enough that a man (without monstrous machinery) could do in his lifetime to change it. Let's walk.

The earth gives a little under our feet, in any season but more so in the spring when water is everywhere and the long road home a vast sea of mud. This particular day is neither spring nor summer, it's unfair to make them separate seasons really when one so quietly and gradually melts into the other: but it's warm, so I'll call the season Warm. Warm is when you don't have to. Warm is freedom. Sometimes this road gets so wet our young friends make the journey to town, where they know of a factory-outlet for rubber boots made in Japan, run by a garrulous character (let's call him Roland) who hails from Quebec. The boots are cheap by the standards of town, sixpence, ten francs, two dollars, a million yen, so they break apart at the seams and are always wanting replacement. That's another lesson we're learning: how everything needs maintenance of one kind or other. A field in this territory would soon become forest unless mowed with a cutter-bar salvaged from scrap and attached to a tractor made many suns ago—back in the time of the great war, a time we cannot recall. And your mind needs maintenance, too, you know: changing the oil every 10,000 miles, an occasional complete overhaul. Mostly we know that all of this would vanish and die the moment we stopped paying attention—so that though these trees grow, this water springs, that moon shines, with no obvious help from ourselves, we are actually in control and making it all happen with the strength of our good intentions and wishes. Just look at that great old fieldstone, for example: it is useful to us, make it hard with the passage of billions of moons so we'll have a stool and a resting-place. Here we've hardly begun, the farm is yet distant, and already we're tired. But the glass hill is steep, it's warm after all, and we've decided we're not in a hurry. Let's rest.

I remember this place. I have sat here since the birth of time. The apple tree, though not far behind, is invisible now, we are bordered all around by towering evergreens, spruce and pine, that hang over the road like a covered-bridge, heavy with snow in winter and sparkling with top-heavy sunshine now. A place in the shade. The road keeps twisting and climbing, so the limits of our vision extend no more than 20 feet. Sitting on the fieldstone, we suddenly realize the din and thunder of our very feet had been drowning out the birds. Sitting still, we can hear them come back to life—unceasing and chatty, they are playing in harmony with the delicate swoosh of a waterfall just up ahead. Tweet, twort, swoosh. Lying down on the fieldstone, we must shelter our eyes from the blinking sun among the needles overhead. I shall sit here, the frog said, until tomorrow. (Or was he a frog after all? It is still only morning and the frogs don't get busy till twilight, when they peep and worp in chaotic percussion all night.) I shall lie here until I am fieldstone, and farmers will come in their overalls, worn down at the seat, and use me for rest.

One of the charms of the place, why deny it, is its emptiness. I mean it's inspiring to be sitting here with you and knowing we are alone—except for the flora and fauna of course, the birds and fishes and deer, squirrels and porcupines, rabbits and coons, and so on. And sun and moon and so on. And heavenly bodies. And so on. But I mean there's no *people* around. We know what would happen if too many people came by—so long so-on! Yet, as unlikely as it is to happen, we certainly would enjoy encountering, say, Old Jesse out hunting for dreams—he lost them *right around here* a long time back. Or Ed with his pipe and red jacket, out walking for reasons of health. (Otherwise driving a jeep, grown up as he is.) Or any of the folks from the farm. Or maybe even Old Man Ripley putting up buckets although it's too late in the season. Or Cathy fetching the runaway Dolly, Jeannie the runaway Janice. Or the fellow with the white beard and walking stick who emerges from the woods just this time of year, looks puzzled at the road, its bareness as planet, not even a fern growing on it, and vanishes heading due north. (He'll be back in the fall.) As I say, we could run into these or other good people, and be glad of the accident: but we probably won't. Some do. To be honest, I'd have to admit to you sometimes it gets pretty lonely. Not often, though. And especially in Warm, we're always surrounded. Are you yet ten? I will be ten next winter, Mother said, but in Warm I shall simply play with the days and examine everything closely. See this leaf? See my toe? See that skunk? Look harder, play rougher, and you'll see an infinity of energy recklessly spent.

Sometimes it can get lonely for a kid. That's why we built the clubhouse. I can't remember when it was I became an orphan, and was out in the cold, but since we've built the clubhouse I have lots of friends and we keep each other warm. We hang around the clubhouse a lot, it's been a grand success you know, for our mothers and dads have yet to find us. Have they given up looking?, I wonder but only when I'm afraid. Other times I know they'll be by for us and we'll all just go home, watch Lassie or something and then we'll have to go back to school. When I grow up I will be able to climb birches. But it *has* been a while since we lost our leaders, and the clubhouses springing up everywhere like ports in a storm. Perhaps it is we who are found, and our parents are lost! But I doubt it. They always *seemed* to know, in their grave fashions, exactly where they were going, not to mention the balance-of-payments deficit, cost of eggs, and likelihood of rain. They wore rubbers, too. But they couldn't be *so* clever if they can't catch up with us!

It would surely be interesting if your mother caught us here right now. She'd say, "Aha! Henry James Morrison, I've been *looking all over* for you! Your soup-n-sandwiches are getting cold and Sister Mary Shillaleah Gonnorhea is about to mark you absent in geography!" Absent in geography! But on the other hand, if your mother could find us *here,* she'd have to come *here,* and then she could just join the club at the house! For *here* is a state of mind, you know. It's not like in the old days when if she found the clubhouse, you could always relocate it in the woods a full block from your house; those woods are full of serious "homes" now with men who didn't get haircuts till their hair grew down to on-their-legs, and ladies who get permanents. No, there is no place to run to from here. I'm making all this up, you see, and Total Loss Farm doesn't really exist, and all the stories about it which I will, in time, unfold for you didn't really happen. At least you can't get there from here, and they happened only in the twilight of my mind. Who can say?

This state of being lost is one of the most delightful and troublesome places I know. So long as we are secure, you see, we can afford it—but when insecurity and paranoia creep in, watch out! Our strongest security is not in stocks and shares or anything foolish and sober like that, but in our certain sense of being watched over and protected from all calamity; our attempt to relate to the environment as part of it rather than as onlookers, for example. Do you understand? Of course you do. It is eminently desirable to have the big space in your head, but only when you absolutely *know* that it'll be all right, God will provide. Some people go to expensive institutions to be sheltered: whether by librium or electrodes-on-the-brain or just throaty talk from the nice or not-so-nice man in the white shirt. How much more practical to be sheltered under the spreading chestnut tree and in your own bed!

Over the crest of the hill, for the first time the road descends—walking downhill for a stretch we can catch our breath. That's why we built the road so, that horses pulling loads up the farm could recuperate from the uphill struggle and, freshened, go on. The road dips down to a wooden bridge crossing a stream of many colors in which pickerel, trout, salmon, tuna, and whales have been spotted by the sharpest of eyes. Most folks see only an occasional small trout or sunfish in this Noname Brook, which leads nowhere, but that is because they are all nearsighted. They wear glasses in the faith that the real, or actual, universe is not the one their own eyes can see, but a standard, universal universe dictated by prescription, or politics. You'd certainly be welcome to hang on to your specs here, but this is a place where you *could* take them off without fear of ridicule or violence to your body. Without my glasses, the brook becomes a dazzling pulsating streak of sunlight across the earth, ill-defined and like the great Source difficult to watch for long. They say it can blind you, but how to know which things you might better be blind to? Our great adventure after all is in searching for something not only better but new, nothing less than the next step in the evolution of the race, which may be somewhere we've been before. It goes in spells. And in racing toward the New Age, we can't be expected to carry all the dead weight of the past—all the schools, factories, newspapers, jobs, religions, and movements—which would drag us under. Just do whatever comes to mind, do something you hadn't thought of before, it's bound to get you *somewhere*. And you'll then decide whether you like it and where to move on to. We might stay at the brook all day and be perfectly happy, even dangle our toes in the chilly clear water, but me I'm now anxious to get on up to the farm. Coming?

The brook will stay with us right up to the top of the hill, running alongside the road and crossing it several more times—through culverts rather than bridges as it narrows with the increased elevation. A culvert is a cylinder made out of stone which the good fairy comes every 100 years to repair. They're buried beneath us so it's clear no mere mortal could ever have access to one, though it's easy to see the tail-ends as they poke out the sides of the road. Everything that's buried: must converge.

There are two haunted houses where nobody lives, except on specific holidays. You might call them "vacation homes" if you didn't know any better, but I have passed them sun upon moon upon season, always empty always empty, so I know there is something about them which makes them forbidding. It's not they lack soul, but rather they wail with the souls of the dead who fought with the land for a living, and retired under those roofs when they'd given up for the night. It weren't no "vacation." Think of the babies they had, the bottles they nursed, their wives who grew old and complaining, their utter despair of higher expectations, their awareness of being trapped. In a minute we'll see what's become of them in a trim little graveyard, officially full for 200 years. In the meantime, that brown house holds the relics of a family named Billings that failed in the dairy business after He hung himself in the barn. And the red one was Cheever, who once made a fortune bottling this water as medicinal, but lost everything, including himself, in the great epidemic. At the height of the sun, for a moon or two, the ghouls come from the city with whiskey in bottles and babies in vehicles, camp out in these houses, and cook up animal flesh over pits—an annual ritual perhaps designed to placate the restless unhappy who lived here. It is an uneasy time at best, and the crops at the farm have been noticed decidedly wilting until it is over.

At the farm, we are lost and thus always on vacation. Vacancy is the better part of fertility. In nothing there's plenty for everybody.

Call me a simpleton, but I don't understand how a house can be a "vacation home" unless you live there all the time. If vacation to them is a novelty, how can it also be home? I am nearly always home, and very unhappy when I wander. Home-in-my-head is forever unexplored, challenging, unfathomable; foreign parts too often drearily predictable and concrete.

"Stay home," Henry again, "and see the world!"

The graveyard looms. It sits at the foot of a hill capped and crested by the road. Surrounded by fieldstone carried by horses and laid by men for a fence, it's a beautiful compost-heap out of which nothing but our aspirations grows. Myself, I'd prefer to be burned. Let's look at the stones: "Here lies Lionel Billings, who roared in his sleep, fathered ten children, died in winter." And his wife Julia, who did what she ought've. Their son Amos, overtaken by a putrid fever. Old Lionel, like Shakespeare, thought he was leaving his mark. His furrows are forest now, yet we remember. How could we ever forget? But names aren't important, nor even the deeds, it's just that the graveyard belongs to the farm, and to you. We've absorbed it. On to the pond.

I'll never forget the summer we built the pond. There's a very adequate Beaver Pond right down in the woods, but it's not on sacred territory, and its "owners" are all grown up. That's what convinced Mark to lead the pond-building brigade, and everyone helped. First we cleared the woods with hatchets, axes, and hand saws, just as the beavers would do if *they* had chosen the spot. Then we laid the felled lumber over the stream for a dam. The construction was sound but unless beavers came we'd have to repair it at least once a Warm. The water rushing right at our feet, past the clubhouse and down the mountain is powerful enough to knock you over if you stand in it. Then splash! you'd go flying and come up soaked and smiling, right near the place where M and I drowned the kittens. There were 30 kittens in all but we drowned only five, who were sick. They mewed and shrieked and I could see through the brook clear as atmosphere, and cold enough to numb my clenched fists, that their every attempt for air was rewarded with water. It took a long time for them to die.

It was that first summer, too, that Don drowned in our pond. He had just come up from New York, where his job as a hip newspaper-man had all but destroyed him. He knew too much, and even a burning desire to rediscover himself in the woods couldn't erase all the inside information. Unlike the kittens, though, he died graceful as a swan, as if that pond had been built as his chariot to home. Since then we haven't gone swimming in it very much, though the beavers finally came—a year late—and improved on our work. Somebody built a yellow boat and adorned it with magical symbols, when this stream was the Nile and he figured sooner or later an infant or corpse would need some craft to float down in. The boat has been moored ever since on a bed of black-eyed Susans, and is always half-full of rain water. The history of the place can't diminish its beauty or peace, though, and on occasion I still come down here to strip off my clothes and let the sun do what it will with me, splash in the water when it gets too hot to handle, run my fingers through my hair, and in general love myself. I'd thought often of loving somebody else here, my fellow man for instance, for the pond is sheltered from view of the road, that rare and precious thing: a private place. But making love by the pond-where-Don-drowned just wouldn't do, though Crane and I came here once naked together and whiled away afternoon just pleased with gazing on each other. We were young, and beautiful. We heard no intrusive sounds all day, and fingered blades of grass and blew on milkweed while conversing.

It is awfully hard to be nine once you'll never see nineteen again. I am never quite free of the forces attempting to make me grow up, sign contracts, get an agent, be a man. I have seen what happens to men. It is curious how helpless, pathetic, and cowardly is what adults often call a Real Man, who wears his balls like a badge instead of a secret, a symbol rather than real mystery; his courage reduced to encounters with the boss. He worries. He is responsible without being responsive, and proud of his penchant for taking the rap though he knows he is powerless to create the act. If that is manhood, no thank you. I would rather know nothing of the cold cruel world I will someday just have to deal with, same as everybody else. Children take life by the short hairs. They are the real Makers of life, they believe in it. And all of us know how it was, so each of us can remember. Innocence is our only possible hope. I am saying this just for you, I am trying to help you. Because even the pond where Don drowned can be a tabernacle to me, that's how easily children forget; and sacred to you, too, some body of water in darkest forest where you can always go to be whole.

To get back on the road from the pond, we'll have to push aside twigs and underbrush, trample some black-eyed Susans, cut to the left under the vast old spruce tree (its bark makes excellent chewing gum), watch out for magic mushrooms and special herbs, finger a crystal stone, turn it in the early eastward light, dig how the brown earth of early Warm readies now to get green as clover, how the naked shuddering trees now bud, now burst, now silently absorb the sunlight. Holy holy holy the field between pond and road, where the cow or horse might graze in July, now just a sepia, amber, early bed for our lazy lovemaking. What have we done in our lives to deserve such profuse blessing of God? Nothing clearly but luck and the sure protection of Mother Honeywell over her own—but I'm saving her for later. Stick around. The seasons surround us and provide endless variety of good scenemaking but *this* is the nicest of all! (Guess what, we say that about *all* of them!)

A nasty big man came from the town 20 miles and 2,000 feet down the line with an offer to alter the seasons. For a fee, he would make the winter warm as toast—burnt toast—and the summer cool as cucumber. And make rain out of propane, hot or cold, at the flick of a limp wrist. Mother it was to first see the devil out the door, send him back to his 20-mile-gone hell of human making. "Go open a checking account! Go tempt the lost souls of the poor!" she shouted, wiping wholewheat flour hands on a cotton apron, and while Brother Mike got out the axe, old Mr. Trouble went whooping down the mountain with his tale between his ears. How they would jaw on this in town, at the mill, at the Daily Tatler office, and how in vain their jawing always will be! For sounds of that sort are long drowned by the wind before they reach our door. In my former life, I too was guilty of daily slander, for I spoke of associates and friends rather than faeries and gods.

Our next stop: the picnic grove. Pygnic grove. This is the great accomplishment of Lucien Packer who died mumbling of February some years ago and left the place to us. He didn't get much else done —o he would have been one of us, given the chance, I am sure—a sharp constructive mind nestled comfortably in that slow and slothful exterior—but he built one hell of a jeep out of the junkpile and this here picnic grove of stone, oak, and pine. The building supplies hereabouts grow, so to speak, on trees: or else in the rocky and infinitely solid soil. So: here are three stone fireplaces, long solid tables unrotted by exposure to the elements, swings and slides for the kiddies (that's us), and the same old bubbling brook behind. The trees are all pine, thick so it's ever in the shade here, even at Labor Day noon. Mother and I come here to gather the needles in smelly brown burlap sacks, to sprinkle like faery-dust on the blooming potatoes, that you can't even see till they're ready: but when the grainy greenery comes up to your knees and spreads out drooping as wide as your chest, then pull 'em up! We sleep on the needles, too, they are the softest of all, and in winter they're better than newsprint for starting the fire.

Packer was descended of Mother Honeywell, and his ancestors operated a tavern here for the brawling good boys of independent mind. They took no shit from General Washington, King George, or the Mohawks. They took no shit, and had none to give; and lost their precious independence. Clothed as they made it in a political state, they could only lose it. It was a daydream from start to finish, as politics is rhetoric and idle fancy. They might better have striven to be free in their heads, but their heads were doubtless clouded with Lucien the First's incredible home-brew, not unlike our Junior's château, tromped with good foot (the one without *tzoris*), and fermented through all of October. All these things *do* go on. And on.

The first pygnic in the grove was, for us, a dream induced by Silly Cy Bin, who came to lighten our load. We were just up from the cities, it was August, we were roasting our dogs (sins of the fathers) and drinking beer of Milwaukee, eating chips of potatoes of Idaho, we'd barely arrived when the first test began. A jeepful of concerned friends arrived with the news they were coming to get us. Who? Why the men of town with their shotguns and red hats of course. Why? Because we were foreigners on their magic and sacred soil, and they feared what spells we were casting. On the hill, which is the highest in town. Some said get out John's old musket, others let's go hide, but Silly Cy Bin said only: "Feel: the wind under the sun across the shady pine grove. Hear: bubbling rushing water behind the wall of trees. Smell: the needles making mulch and all agreen aliving. Fear: not." Who came that night was just a bunch of wildass high-school kids whose dads had labored hard to make a go of life in these great and cold hills and who were we to come and make it look so easy? Is it easy? To begin again from rude nature who learned from phones and subways? I would like to tell you it's easy, I'm so enthused even

now with the Life, but I'd be lying to you if I did, and giving you no
help at all in the bargain. It's not easy, dear one, to live this modern,
anachronistic Life, but it's great and grave and vibrant, miraculous
and holy, serene and ecstatic, lovely and loving in a full, rich, finely
textured way with *details* and *quality* and *character*. Like the swell-
ing rolling shaded pygnic grove where trees are free of harm—the
grove of culinary delights which Lucien built, wise fellow, for his
vast and helter-skelter country family, spread over three townships,
to come together when? On the Fourth of July! When crackers boom
and the beer flows free, not because grandfather lost out to General
Washington, but because the plants are all in, haying yet to begin, all
the stores and factories and mills closed. Because it's always Yes to
everything in Warm.

(Intermission: late April now. Raymond here. The neighboring
farm of young refugees has just burned to the ground. It is two miles
to there, and the road all but impassable. The men of town in their
red hats came in a caravan, the Volunteer Fire Department, not such
ogres after all but trying to help save the children. We climbed in a
heap in the back of a jeep to push it and lift it over the slimy spring
mudroads, through the mild night, under the shadow of Mount
Muste, and lit by a full moon encircled with mile-wide ring.

(Too late. Too late. Four of them dead, four others burned, the
house gone, the survivors barefoot and silent. Would they come
home with us to beds and coffee and a real brick chimney? No they
would stand and stare at the ruins, rooted rooted rooted to the earth,
till morning. And then?

(Can you remember? what chances children will take? how they
come here because out-there drove them away, and are rooted? Remember then Josh, remember Mitch, remember Regina, remember
Peter who had never even shaved. When you build a chimney, start
at the bottom, insert a flue lining, make it double-walled brick if you

can, clean it twice a winter, always be careful. If you have no chimney, and are using stovepipe, clean it once a month for creosote. If you have electricity, check the wiring and get circuit-breakers. If you don't have it, use kerosene lamps rather than candles. If you must use candles, put them on plates or stones, and put them out before you go to sleep.

(And what of the four long bodies from the neighboring pasture? O now we must be stronger and saner than ever, I must write truer than ever, you must be more than ever my friend. We must take care of each other, now that we are without. Without. I have spent a good deal of the evening in tears, but enough now I'll go on scribbling. We have yet to discover what it is beyond God and planet which makes the Life worth living, and why there is no going back.)

There is a secret way to get to the farm from the picnic grove, it's a little harder but well worth the effort. We go behind the grove, you see, over the brook, up through the forest to the sugarbush, down the old logging road to the orchard, then across the enormous noon field to the clubhouse. Can you remember all that? The path through the woods is steeper than Pike's Peak, we'll run and leap and fall into beds of leaves, stop for air, puff and pant, watch the road and the grove disappear way, way beneath us, we are going higher than ever before, we won't stop until we are in the almighty sugarbush, on top of the world. Why are we so desperate to get there? Because the sugarbush, a clearing in the woods surrounded by tall maples who give annually of their blood to support us, and ask nothing in return, is the Source and the secret. If we could live in the sugarbush, as the old porcupine and the fleet does do, and be the first to catch the sun, the last to relinquish winter's white carpet, the center of energy and cathedral of meaningless unending explosive and uncontrollable life, we would be silent and wise and worry no more over fire or hunger or war. We would stand, and stand, though Berkeley is burning and love grows cold, and wait for summer to turn to fall and have no need of trifling companionship or vain gestures. Will this story be printed on somebody's sugarbush? Hopefully then this might be the last, and the best, story of all. Tieing up the loose ends is yet another way to get free.

The ascent to the sugarbush is hardest the first time you do it. Once here, we are tempted never to leave, though it's all downhill to get back and the forest is spooky. The children once had the notion of building a shack here, but of course it's impossible: the land is too steep, the lone clearing too precious, the forest too dense to admit even a jeep carrying building supplies and tools. The maples themselves would make sinewy logs for a cabin, but how could we slice down the goose, who so relish the golden eggs? The syrup of March is pure natural energy, it slides down our throats with the ease of the atmosphere. A big round storage tank sits in the clearing, dumbly awaiting the sap, which flows down to the road and into a second tank through through several thousand feet of clean hardware store pipe. At least when the pipe doesn't break, the tank leak, or the season abruptly end. O well, it takes time, as I said, to make any progress, and we insist on the right to make all the mistakes at least once. And commit the unforgivable sins. We figger everybody's entitled to one unforgivable act per year, how's that? We can neither forgive or forget it, but chalk it up to the great adventure of living, and go on.

A dooty girl came from the city once, her name was Marguerite or Rita or something sexy like that, and I took her up here. It was an impossibly difficult seduction, by the time she had cursed the steep rises and ripped her dress on the bushes and fallen into the streams, she was hardly ready to lie with me on the dirty ground. A dooty girl is the kind that knocks you out with a swagger, and seems indestructible till you take her to God. Walking down some avenue, she goes

"Doot Doot Doot Doot" in perfect rhythm of hips. Ah well, it's not for everybody.

So we never could build in the sugarbush, try as we might—there are simply some places where man is forever a visitor, welcome perhaps in daylight but frightened by ghouls and lost bobcats at night. The sounds of the forest are awesome and strange, and even your ear, new to the place, could pick up the chatter of animals, loose moaning of the wind, soft crying of children who wandered from tepees and huts and died in the woods in the days before time. The deed to the farm says: "so-many acres of houses and land, and a parcel of forest where no man belongs." We knock on the door of the forest before we go in, it's only polite.

Down, now on the logging road, alongside a fieldstone fence now useless for fencing out anything—even the arthritic Dolly, a Jersey, could leap it with ease, her neck bell brassily clanking, if she chose to bother. This old road leads, most of the time, to the orchard— from which, if we're lucky, the farm may be visible. Some days, it simply disappears, melts away so to speak, and not even us can find it. That's one of Mother Honeywell's tricks. The legend is that when the farm disappears, the children have all died and gone to heaven. Once, while up in the orchard, we saw ourselves confusedly searching for the farm. "We're not home!" we shouted to our distant bodies, and the echo made the very Mount Muste quiver. Our bodies went away then, back to the womb I suppose, while our souls took their places on the highest limbs of the orchard.

For the orchard, unlike the sugarbush, is a vantage-point. It crests the top of the openest hill and hayfield, too steep for crops but perfect for rolling and sliding and falling. When the farm is there at all —as it is today—we can see it entire and miniature, like play-farm plastic toys you set up on the linoleum while mommy is busy at dishwashing. We can see the long shed with its stallsful of funny red

Volkswagens, the big old barn, majestic and crimson, with hens and rooster enpenned, a chestnut mare named Janice, the doleful and true-blue cow Dolly, a very silly white goat, some dogs who are heading up here as fast as they bound (which means we've been spotted and like it or not we'll have to go down and fall into the family, we'll have to take chances), the clubhouse itself, rich brown, blue roof, blood-of-the-Lamb red door to signify we're God's chosen people, may the butchers of boyhood pass us by in the night. Beyond this barnyard setting, at once Norman Rockwell and Dali, the long flat field where corn and potatoes, peas and melons, tomatoes and onions and love all grow, with the help of some well-chosen chants. And more stately apple trees, berries of every variety, herbs and spices *cultivées,* pears and flowers and hay and suddenly Mountains, one on another, stretching as far as tomorrow and yearning to play with the clouds like dragons. And sky, big blue and spherical, and sun overhead us directly, for we've gotten here precisely at chlorophyll noon, in time for our lunch.

And what of the orchard itself, from which all these wondrous and forgotten treasures are luckily visible, despite what we know from our checkbooks and media? It hangs red and yellow and heavy and dazzling with: peaches.

I promise you all these things are so, if you will let them be. Regardless of anything.

Michael is softly playing guitar in the kitchen, the soul of the farmhouse. He is lost in the music, caressing the strings as they spontaneously respond to both his ear and his body. Everything within him is moving, otherwise all is still. It is unpredictable, the kitchen: at noon it might be bustling with bodies moving earth and sky to some new and more appealing arrangement; today we are content to let it be. The children are gathered in the main living room, noiselessly sipping a lentil soup which the Flying Zucchinis, a brother-sister team out of Oregon, have cooked on Home Comfort with a liberal assortment of spices. It could be Mexico and this our midday siesta; let's enjoy it, it can't last for long. Home Comfort is a wood-burning stove, black and grey, six round iron discs on top which are removed with graceful sloping iron handles; and over all, two warming ovens, on which the manufacturer has painted tufts of wheat and sickles. Home Comfort is the trade name of the stove, it probably dates from the 30's, though that's just a guess. It has an oven of course—with an approximate thermometer—which is always too hot on the bottom shelf, too cold on the top. Yet every substantial foodstuff, from rice and salad to cheese soufflés, and daily breads, cakes, and pies, is made here. And once you're tuned into Home Comfort, no other stove will do as well, no other bread be worth its sourdough starter.

The children eat well by any sound standards—they eat what is good for them, what grows in their own backyard, and they never fuss or complain. They are seldom actually hungry though often enough, and especially in winter, they do without much variety in the diet. With milk and cheese from Dolly, eggs from the girls (and occasionally a girl or two), such meat and fish as is given them or as they can kill for themselves, endless fruits and vegetables, and now-and-then shipments of lentils or rice, they are probably healthy as horses. At least they haven't lost *weight*.

They once had a pig, but they killed it. "Kill the pig! Kill the pig!" they shouted, chasing fat Rhoda clear around the orchard and and finally doing her in—cutting and cleaning her, hanging her up to bleed. A terrible controversy then, one of the few I can remember, for some of them stubbornly chewed on lettuce and grains while the others dismembered old Rhoda, shanks and breasts and all, and gleefully ate her up for protein. Which side are you on? It's fair to say, though, that their consumption of meats has been vastly reduced since they came here from God-knows-where. In a million brilliant senses, they can't afford it any more.

Back to the kitchen, where it all begins. (And it ends, of course, in the outhouse—a fancy two-seater, though one of the holes is too small for absolute comfort. Silent's been promising to widen it with his sword for nearly a year now. There's nothing quite like that gentle breeze—or stiff wind, depending on season,—that assaults our rosy behinds from the place where the tarpaper keeps blowing off. Or the biannual shit-burying detail, which everyone joins since nobody could claim to be faultless. We all do our share, to be sure. And let me tell you some pretty weird shit turns up in the course of it—from the conventional you-n-me waste to tools and houkas and the New York Times Arts and Leisure Section.) (I'm sorry to get so distracted, but one thing leads to another.) The kitchen is mostly wood, as is the rest of the house, and bereft of shiny appliances. There is a baking table usually dusty with flour; pots and pans and measuring cups hung from the ceiling; an oak cabinet which Mystic Mark built, housing cracked mugs and assorted blue-chipped dishes, survivors of "sets" now mostly broken, behind his-n-hers latches, a pipe and a sweet embroidered clasp; a 1940 Maytag wringer washer which quit working almost as soon as it got here, but is kept around for aesthetic reasons; tin pails for garbage, separated into Organic and Junk; a sink with chrome faucets; crude pine shelves lined with plants in peat-cups, berries in Mason jars, syrup in cans; huge flour-bin; wood-box to hold the fuel; snarfing refrigerator, its contents up for grabs; sacks of dog food from stores in the town; a shelfful of Epsom Salts, baking soda, aspirin, mercurochrome, and a score of homemade remedies; and twelve neat toothbrushes, all in a row, hanging on nails in the wall. See: we remember to brush after all, though not necessarily after meals. After meals we mostly talk—of life, love, and agriculture, of why the horizon is golden, who broke the chain saw, of how the Red Queen performed six impossible things before breakfast. That sort of conversation is starting now in the living room; let's join it.

Through the pantry with its sacks of onions (the ones that the goat couldn't get), shelves of preserves and soy sauce, Bull Board with offers of rides to the West and imposing notice of debts, light bulb that must be twisted on or off; past the sewing room which looks like your grandmother's; over the New Orleans Bandstand, graced with bulging New Hampshire Porche-poles and a round dining table built on a cider barrel; under the heavy 10-inch beams supporting a loft where poets and madmen and Beanie the Rabbit are all sleeping it off on a big round mattress; to the stage and the Stove, where all who're awake are sitting in tumbledown rockers (every chair is a rocker, and each is broken—the kids love rocking, and know how to deal with the eccentricities of each: in the *green* chair, lean only to the left, etc.) and passing the precious moments after bean-soup lunch together, they are sitting and holding together. There are 24 in all today, the neighboring clubhouse burned down, bringing so many sympathizers and friends, and one came from Ireland, walking all night with his pack on his glowing shoulders. Tomorrow there may be only five or six. But no matter, see: how these folks seem to know one another, to live with each other in uncommon peace and harmony, they seem to accept their fate of being-together like Boystown-in-Hollywood good-hearted kids of the past. They respect each other, or so it seems. They are willing to listen and sit here all day if even a single member of the family has that much to tell. And despite the adventures they'd surely fall into—pirates, Indians, witches, mermaids—outside the door, the well-turned hyperbole or anguished cry of a brother is gripping as well. They really have nowhere to go, which means they can go anywhere they choose. They will play it by ear, and none of them knows what will happen. They would not be surprised if the whole world collapsed on their heads in a minute— for it has in the past. They are the modern family, who are holding together for right-now and forever, because they choose to, and because they are having fun. The minute it got to be a drag, they'd say "fuck it" and walk away! In that, they are loyal to the guiding principles of Total Loss Farm: which was born when the outer society became such a bore, and descended into such thorough decay, they said "fuck it" and went off to live in a world not yet of human making, and see if they couldn't do better. Time will tell. Professors from colleges and writers of paperbacks describe their society as a relief-valve for the unending bullshit of out-there, but the children know nothing of this, they don't go to college and don't read the relevant books. They read faery-tales, of course, and know only that life on the farm has been better to them than any other life they have had.

Michael has gone upstairs to sleep in his San Francisco den. That's one of our rarer fantasies: that someday we'll go to San Francisco, just as the big people do, and give the city another chance. No other city being of course worth consideration. And Michael himself has made three trips to the West since we came here—at least he has vanished three times to reappear a month or two later with a story of San Francisco or Oregon. He came here with Mother but that was of course a long time ago and before we abolished couples. I thought since we'd abolished couples we might as well go all the way and abolish individuals—that's what we're working on now. Each of us still has some secrets: special places where the Monopoly pieces are stashed, a little present for you little girl, etc. etc. It will take some time to get rid of our secrets—without losing the sure knowledge that each of us is Christ Almighty. Independence within dependence is another of the ironies which suddenly make perfect sense in our lives. Of the obvious shit, we've managed to act pretty sensibly— nobody really wants a private car anymore, for example, it gives the machine too much power and sanctity, and the car ends up owning you. So a car is just a car, and you may drive any one you like assuming it *works*. Today, most don't. There's a crippled VW with sunroof (watch out for the gas pedal, it sticks) and a Peugeot lacking only a battery; and of course the Land-Rover on permanent loan from a man in the hollow, and which is full of odd tricks. The bus blew a rod. O well. Food is to be eaten, not saved—though a Dinner Refrigerator is supposedly immune from raiding, and kept for the makings of meals. But it seldom holds anything we could just eat without cooking (and cooking requires building a fire, which requires chopping up wood, which doesn't grow on trees, you know): for the children haven't heard of Devil Dogs, and eating to them is a ritual for which you could spend any time you liked in preparing, without wasting any. As Silent said, food is the whole bloody thing, here or anywhere. They are feeding themselves, and growing the stuff, without any help from charity or Welfare, in order to do so again on the morrow.

You have heard that millions are starving. It is undoubtedly true. Did you know that at least some of them needn't? That is, without more being grown or imported, they could find enough food without leaving home. You have read *Stalking the Wild Asparagus,* so you know. But the starving often don't know or else certain cultural customs prevent them from venturing into something new. Just as I have met grownups who would rather wriggle and suffer than shit in the outhouse, even in Warm, there are others who simply won't eat as we do, who claim that our dinners are just make-believe. They'd sooner go hungry until they can get to the store or the restaurant, where American pseudo-food wrapped up in cellophane is exchanged for hula-dollars. It is all quite bizarre, is it not? In respect to our countrymen, we often feel we are vastly outshone for absurdity—it is they who are freaks, really and truly, while we are altogether straight and wholesome. (Were the truth known, we are shameless reactionaries, harking to our past as the key to our future.) The same may be said of domestic habits, how the unwritten law that a man and his wife and their children together constitute a separate and closed society in their home can only be called a perversion of ancient human practice, if not "nature." And how the genetic family so often is riddled with gulfs, so that father and son, or brother and sister, really know nothing of each other's life and mind, and care less.

What remains to discover is why the kids here can look on each other as brother and sister, protect each other from all harm, and cast their material lots together without concern for the fraudulent privacies of yesterday: why have they not quarreled over money, how can they live all in a heap, do they not find each other's manner offensive, never fight over a woman or man to love as property, why

150

have they no ambition? Is it because they cannot pursue the material goals which their parents before them succeeded in reaching? No, not really; but because their own goals and lives are *truly* material, not the fake comforts of Buick and Sylvania but the richness of soil and the texture of oatmeal bread: the children are not idealists and politicians, children never are, but real hedonists: they want the best of everything, and at Total Loss Farm that is the standard. And they love each other, I suppose, because they enjoy it—everyone knows how much harder and less rewarding it is to hoard and envy; trust the kids to take the easiest way out. The easiest and only way out is forever and always *through,* that is another of their sayings. It requires, this love, a death of the ego. Who me? you reply. No I they exclaim.

I am mixing my pronouns. Don't worry, it doesn't matter.

It is time we got acquainted with the denizens of this ancient and hallowed room, with its bird cage and sombrero, library of everyone's college requirements, cracked and wounded Baby Grand on a ten-foot-high platform. Michael, who went to sleep, milks cows in the early dawn for a farmer who fell off his silo, cursed his luck, fought the agents of the bank in the town, and finally lost his land. Old Farmer Ripley, who took it too seriously. Michael was born of a certain collision of stars in the West, carried here on top of the wind, floated down like a feather. Mark over there came out of the eastern ocean—washed ashore, he got himself up and started walking west, toward the mountains. His passion is building in wood; the things he creates are seldom finished, his work is forever in progress, but it lasts for a thousand Warms without sign of decay. Mother isn't really our mother, of course, she got that name from being the largest of ladies, a poet and maker of love affairs and bagels. She lives in the chickenhouse, where tea is forever on, and accommodates visitors one by one in her bottomless heart and hearth. Mother is the top banana in my grocery, since long before either of us was born; she came here with me on a wing and a prayer, as the old-time storyteller said. Sneaky Pete, alias Silent, was found abandoned in a pretzel factory, left in the dough bin, and came to us in a package marked Fragile: Perishable: Handle With Care: Via Air Mail. He is believed to be born of the gypsies, he wears a red kerchief over his curls and is likely to fly away to foreign fields without notice, returning at crimson sundown to fashion a strudel of Swedish apples, cinnamon from Persia, raisins of France.

Tricky Dick is a boy of Dixie, whose spinal cord and nervous system responds like a fine-tuned G-string to the pluckings and beatings of outrageous fortune. They threw him out of the nursery for writhing and bopping to old Otis Redding. Since then he's been sliding up and down the seaboard looking for hot licks and temporary shelters. He's been here now for 600 years, so it looks like he's staying. He's swarthy and skinny and strangers he meets will likely as not address him in Spanish. To which he replies "mañana," the only word he knows. Junior came up the hard way, peddling Record-Americans in Scollay Square, sweeping chimneys in winter, living huddled in rags in the dark chambers of a boy's mind who doesn't know why or where. The time he slit his wrists: but that was before: it was because he thought he was alone. Now he enjoys playing Chico, the curly-headed gagman who comes up with the bacon and serves the spirits to one and all on a tray. He got here through Mark, who found him wandering the coast in winter, and together they built a shack. When the owner of the ocean came to chase them away, they ended up here. Junior, for all he's been through, has learned the incredible secret: he never tells a lie. Not even a fib. He figures, I know, that the worst things in life grow out of folks' fooling each other with gestures and customs and how-de-dos that cover their deepest hostility. Watch out for Junior, he's likely to tell you something you don't want to hear, merely because it's true. We love him madly.

Next comes Badass, who came here with Moonbeam, now heavy with child of Shining Youth. This trio has been dancing since the band began. Badass, despite his name, is all heart: within the family he could deny you nothing you needed: outside of it he peckulates the world. Another of our ancient wise sayings: gentlemen *peckulate*, ladies *pullulate*. (*To peckulate: to plunder the store of the State, embezzle pecunia, to encounter and battle with material forces, to provide. To pullulate: to teem with newborn life, to make something new out of basic material, to burst and warmly explode with a million new runaround creatures, to accept and transform.*) "Peck and Pull"—like Taj the rooster, who keeps the girls in embryos, which keep the children in protein. Isn't it simple? Anyway Badass walks with a swagger befitting a man of the world, which is raised to the level of parody when he's at home, where you don't need to make an impression. When the spirit moves him, which is often, he becomes like a baby, spontaneous, excited, carried away with rushes of indelible impressions riotous life is piling on his mind. Then he will fashion incredible schemes, flailing his arms as he unwinds the fantasy; or quietly, trembling, tell of a miracle that's happening to him, how God is after his ass, and everything up in the air. At times like these, he's the youngest of all. Moonbeam was a born pullulator, and counterpart of Badass, a raven-haired angel. She is sometimes called Wendy. Hardly a lost boy has not fallen in love with her, her miracle and gift is in how she has extended herself to all of them at once. A soft caress, a kind word from Moonbeam, and even the bitterest heart, bereft perhaps of its heritage and wondering whether his folks have forgotten him, will be calmed and sleepy. Lovely Moonbeam watches over us when we are most vulnerable, in the long hours before dawn, and lays her cooling silky palm on the most fevered brows. By morning we have forgotten what visions of carcasses were scaring us, and our nicer dreams rise to the surface like cream. Shin-

153

ing Youth came along on a white horse from the far-away tribes of Florida. He is blonde and soft-spoken, and a perfect gentleman though fewer in years than any of the rest of us; and attends to his chores—weaving, printing, binding, sewing, cooking, growing, keeping his beloved—with attention to exquisite detail. His heart is a teakwood box, easily broken, especially by Moonbeam. Then he flies away to the real world—California, Ohio, Canada—and only the healing of time, sometimes less than a week but it always seems an eternity, will allow him to re-enter the group dream.

And have I ever told you of Tall Foreigner? Of all the boys, he is the largest, skinny and long he bends like a pipe cleaner in a thousand different directions at once, and the other children sometimes poke fun at him for it. But no matter, for he enjoys playing the fool, he senses in the hideout and the happy gay mannerism of the Life a seed of pathos and tragedy, perhaps even evil; he is intent on keeping everyone's spirits up and minds off the morbid possibilities—how they have come here to die, for example—and to do so, he plays his flute, gyrates his body, kicks out his feet, and tries to get everyone to join his masque. Tall Foreigner, it is rumored, was the son of a man of great power, a Defense Minister of one of the allied states, but that is his secret of course and it hardly matters here, though I've sometimes wondered at the specter of an international incident at Total Loss Farm! The others call him Foreigner not because he is not flesh of their blood, but because his accent and posture suggest a world so far away, beyond the farthest mountains and continents removed, as if he has come farthest over the planet, and at greatest expense, to join their play. He is also mad, they whisper, especially when his mood turns dark and his eyes turn south and across the great waters and nobody knows exactly what is on his mind; but they have never feared him, even for an instant. Despite everything, theirs is a world of uncommon security within.

And of course we can't forget the Flying Zucchinis, Jimmy and Julia, whose acrobatics and lithe adjustment to all the newest concerns of the farm cannot disguise their rockbound, almost Latin, faith in some basic morality and belief which is rooted too deep in the past to be comprehensible to their young minds. They as much as any people I know hold the sun and moon and stars as influence and the earth they walk as temple and altar; and in their ministering to the farmfolk, even making soup or heaping a compost-pile or changing a tire on the bus, they are walking sanctuaries and example of the divinity in us all.

And there are so many others. Goldenrod wears flowers in her breast, comes from Hollywood, where her daddy fashioned shoot-em-up Westerns for the entertainment of tens of millions, but which could not in the long run hold the attention of real children for more than a moment before they would insist on making shoot-em-ups and adventure stories of their own lives. So Goldenrod vanished from L.A. to wander central Mexico unarmed and ill-prepared for the harsh advances which may be made on a girl-orphan in that lawless place. Until a kindly tourist snatched her up, and they raced together for a splitsecond escape from the awful inevitability, just as in the final frame the virgin always retains her honor and the would-be rapist slinks back to his freight car, or bar-room. Goldenrod has always had that pure and lofty quality, almost gorgeous detachment, though of course her coin is cast in the same fountain. The others sometimes wonder whether she has stepped out of the movies, *Cinderella* perhaps, for her beauty so often seems out of this world. She did have a favorite friend, her young man, who though he is the soul of gentility and good nature, and earnest beyond the others in his attempts to make sense and good practice out of agricultural matters, somehow got the name of Ramrod: this because he was stem to her petal for so long, and because his sheer physical strength is so awesome, his shoulders wide enough for the greatest of weights. When the kids play at games, shy and grinning Ramrod always wins, unless he humbly concedes a point or two to the opposition to avoid its feeling bad, for he is a little embarrassed at his own corporal capacity. When Jeannie, the blond schoolgirl in pinafore and pigtails, was drowning in the quick currents of the Pumping Station pond down the road, it was Ramrod alone who could snatch and rescue her innocent body from the waves; and you can imagine how much a hero the others held him then!

There are also two girls whose special talent is in making pictures and pretty things to hang on the walls and be admired and wondered-over by the others. Thus they leave reminders of their delicious femininity all about the house, and give the place more sense of home, or delicate balance between the sexes. They are as different as night from day. Stella, or Star, looks on the bright side, paints and draws such scenes from the farm as make the others infinitely grateful in the heart-of-hearts that time and space has brought them here; and in her unceasing good cheer, is as important to the household as the weather: which is saying something. Stella is as firm and reliable as the very foundations on which our new minds are built, and we feel we can turn to her bottomless well of love. The spring that don't run dry. The Lady from Oklahoma, to the contrary, seems always tormented and at her wits' end to bring the loose strands of life together. Her love is, of course, no less generous than Stella's, but the others sometimes feel they ought to look out after her welfare rather than ask for a lift from her; for she will go forth like Lucia di Lammermoor in her silk nightgown, barefoot in the cruel snows of March, to seize the moon in her hair. Her work, like Stella's heart, leaves the children speechless, and I could not even attempt to describe to you in mere words how this great lady interprets Total Loss Farm for them. When the Lady from Oklahoma comes round, for she is a wanderer, the children know they will be treated to a vision of themselves which makes them bigger even than they can realize. And then, with just a little bit of foolish pride, they stick out their chests and say how imponderable and wondrous their lives are, and are grateful that no schoolmarm or textbook shall ever be able to put them down in chapter, verse, and index.

Let me see, who have I left out? Thousands. There is Pain Himself, the only truly humble one of us, who believes he can do nothing very competently but will, we know, rise to the highest and noblest place of all, perhaps save the life of our child, when the proper moment arrives. And Coleen, who saw her contribution in terms of sacrifice for the commonweal, so tender was her melancholy Catholic schoolgirl heart. And Learner, who was always a Loner, and scared us briefly when he seemed all powerful to bring the Sunshine into our kitchen and, presumably, to deny it as well. And John, who learned to fly once he got over some silly notions about propriety, correct grammar, the importance of saving the world of strangers.

We *are* saving the world, of course, as the world for us extends to the boundaries of Total Loss Farm and the limits of our own experience; and Total Loss Farm is everywhere now, perhaps under your own rhubarb patch if you looked at it a little closer, and our experience all that anyone could hope to know of life. We were born and raised by parents who loved us at least until they lost us to a certain high-pitched whistle in the wind which they had gotten too old to hear; we work at maintaining ourselves, though our shared labor is seldom very taxing, for it takes little enough work to make plants grow, most of it is out of our hands, and our relationship to the work one of direct gratification and reward, as children insist on; we have children of our own, though they are fully peers by the time they've learned to eat and eliminate without physical help, and soon become more our masters than our students; and we die, sometimes in sulphurous flames, dramatic and shocking, other times silent and mysterious like the gone children wandering Europe with scenes of the parents engulfed in atrocity scrawled across their minds, but never to be spoken: "I come from Auschwitz, or Hué, or Boston, my father was shot for believing in God and hangs limp forever in front of our home as a reminder to the others; my mother was sold to the grim green soldiers for their sport, and my brother to be used as a woman; I escaped the country of the somnambulent and blind on the back of a wolf who prowled the ruins and took pity on me; I have come here to begin again."

Our parents must wonder where we are, this story is, as much as anything else, an attempt to fill them in, but it grows harder and harder to speak. Fortunately, it grows simultaneously less necessary. I have clothes on my back, though they are old, and a roof over my head and food for my belly. In this, I am luckier than many. I am surrounded by people who would give their own lives in defense of mine, for they know we will make it together or not at all. I wish to be reconciled with all of my enemies, and to live on the planet and glory in peaches to a ripe old age. I am willing to help you as much as I'm able, as a single person can help another, not as a movement or government can help a mass. I may ask for some help from you as well. If you come to my house with love in your heart and there's room for one more—for there isn't always—you may know I will feed you and house you for the night, if you need it. You may see me walking from town to town with my thumb outstretched to the highway, seeking a lift: don't pass me by.

You have seen me everywhere. I am not asking for the vote. I do not seek to be represented. I do not seek to tear down your buildings or march on your castle or sit at your desk. I am interested neither in destroying what you have put up nor in gaining control of your empire. I demand nothing, and nothing is my inheritance. I live in the world, in the woods, with my friends, where not many people come by and the planet is entire and friendly; we like to be left alone except by those who can help. You can help by giving the planet, and peace, a chance. I ask only that you treat yourself right, give yourself the best of everything; and in so doing, you will be acting for me as well. If you can't stop, at least wave as you go by. Slow down, perhaps stop working: you'll find the time for everything you really want to do.

Who am I? In the world of the farm, I am Grampaw, who still finds himself able to deliver of such bombastic lectures as this, thinks he has lived through such madness and chaos, such orgasm and ecstasy, that he has some lessons to give, sleeps with the dogs. I am a fool. I am also Pan, who does in Captain Hook with a sweep of his wooden sword: saying: I am youth! I am joy! I am freedom!

Though the warm sun overhead has moved from directly above the orchard to a westward tilt that covers, now, the garden and is aiming hard for the Mountains on the horizon, yet the full breadth of afternoon remains as the children file out their red door, followed by dogs and cats and the goat, who had inadvertently been allowed in the house in a moment when everybody's guard was down. Rosemary, though soft and loving with her helpless eyes—which say she understands perfectly—has the unfortunate biological tendency to shit and piss without regard to carpets and bedspreads, and to knock over kerosene lamps with a playful butt, which, like Mrs. Murphy's cow in Chicago, could signal the end of the farm. So she is made to wait in the barn and the yard, day and night, for the people to emerge from their clubhouse and respond to her bleating with pats on the head and encouraging words. It is, of course, not so bad for her now that it's warm, but in that she is not different from us, who revel in sunlight and are always willing to stop what we're doing for a torpid roll in the high green grasses. Despite the brightness of the day, too, the moon is out full and wrinkled over the cupola that Mark built for a lookout on top of the barn. We are east of the sun now, and west of the moon, we are everything in between.

The farm is never short on domestic animals, they are as much a part of the movie, or more, than the kids themselves. It started with cats, ten in all (only five left now), then moved into dogs, the goat, Janice the mare and her only-born foal who died of RH blood deficiency, then Dolly and Beanie the Rabbit and Clit the Turtle and Rhoda and Priscilla, the Parallel Pigs, and Taj and His Girls who cut-cut all day while He crows at his own cunning step. Each of the animals serves some useful purpose, if only to bark at the approach of a stranger and give us fair notice to put on a smile (when it's possible); but the children would keep them around, feed them and all, just for the sake of their friendship. They are always considering what to get next, some say that sheep are practical and the field does need mowing, while others dream of a mule with his ears popping out of a straw hat, or a pet raccoon to scrounge in the garbage, or a parrot to screech obscenities. The level of animal life in the yard and the house adds a fresh dimension to their passage of time on the planet, and since they've discovered it they believe they could hardly live otherwise in the future. What would be left of life on the planet when a man could not keep a dog? We have heard, in our worst moments, of towering cities where dogs are unwelcome and millions of people either do without them entirely or beat them into parlor-chair submission, for the streets are not safe for animals. It doesn't take too much intelligence to figure out the logical conclusion of *that,* if you're still into logic.

Tall Foreigner adopted the attitude that he simply wouldn't go where his dog, The Black Booger, could not be at home. That great decision has kept him on the farm ever since—for the times that the Booger went to town, he narrowly avoided catastrophe, and of course he would not be allowed to cross the great waters, owing to customs. Though these restrictions at first took their toll on Tall Foreigner, the Booger seemed delighted with it all, and developed a shiny long coat of black-and-orange and never seemed bored; he smiled in the face of the weather, made love to Mamoushka in heat, hunted chipmunk and muskrat, fathered beautiful children, ran around aimlessly in pursuit of psychedelic butterflies, nipped at the heels of the horse, and once even challenged a wild bull which steamed and thundered across our pasture. We watched him and the other dogs, decided to take ourselves down a peg and live on their level. They obviously know more than we do about how to get on.

The dogs at the farm, like the people, simply belie all the ancient beliefs—they do not by nature have fights, for example, nor form packs (though they have on occasion hunted for meat in the forest, and who are guilty we to deny them?). They all have the habit of falling down, rolling on their backs, and wagging their tails for a belly-rub whenever anyone approaches. And though they bark for arrivals, none of them has ever been known to bite At Total Loss Farm, we are defenseless because we have nothing to defend and nobody could take nothing away from us. If we are strong in our souls and together in our minds, what swarthy invader could harm us? The children say Mother Honeywell, for all her mischief, watches over the place and gives it such powerful vibrations that not even those who think they would *like* to could ever succeed in attempts to hurt us; and though we will die in our time, like Mother herself we'll be buried under this soil, and remain through all famine and war, weather and plague, remain on Total Loss Farm from our pies in the sky, and haunt it. Indeed, we have been here all along.

Mamoushka, the Nice Big Dog, is massive in frame and entirely white, we call her the sweetest snatch in the county since dogs come from everywhere when she's in heat and children cannot resist her. She knows the territory better than we could hope to, and except when the foodstuffs run low in the winter, and she growls for her supper, she's always serene. She always has pups on the summer solstice, who follow her gentle titties about the yard, like a parade of white magic, and nothing sober or evil or despairing can ever penetrate her calm, for she refuses to listen to reason. And don't forget K-K-K-Katy, the irrepressible puppy, of whom it is sung:

When the m-m-m-moon shines,
Over the mountain,
There'll be c-c-c-CaCa on the kitchen floor!

All of these, people and animals, are in the sunlit yard now, and it is afternoon in Warm, it is summer. In summer, each day is a microcosm of all the seasons: dawn is spring, afternoon summer, twilight is fall, and evening is winter: evening, even in Warm, has enough of a chill and its darkness so thorough and inky, that our bodies tell us it is cold, and we should retire to the womb for the night. But now it is time for adventures, and the children are scattering all over the planet, in every direction they are running to see what is going on. We might follow any one of them, how will we ever decide? Ramrod is making for the garden, for instance, with a hayrake over his shoulder, he said earlier he would mulch the tomatoes and clean the pasture spring, perhaps he will encounter a brownie or gremlin or even a skunk; Mother is circling the barn and heading for the chicken coop, where Taj with his many-colored coat is making happy noises; Stella is off to the pine grove, she will follow the signs; the Flying Zucchinis with towels and biodegradable soap will go for a swim in the pond, taking Mamoushka for company; Junior and Mark are going to walk in the woods with old maple-sugar buckets to fill with blueberries (it's early for blueberries but they're counting on luck); Goldenrod is down to the hollow for fishing; Michael is building a Dune-Buggy more for the hell of it than any desire to drive; Jeannie is combing-down Janice the mare; Silent is building a new house for Rosemary, who has followed Ramrod into the onion-patch again, where Shining Youth has gone to chase her and, laughing, stumble, and fall over pumpkins quietly growing like our fat benign heads; Moonbeam, of course, is with Dolly; and Badass is up on the roof, fixing a leak. Some others are still in the house, figuring it all out, and you and I are sitting on elm stumps circling a campfire-place in the middle of the yard, dazed by all of this growing and running and leaping, wondering if it's not all a dream.

Dreamily, then, to the garden. The growing season is long enough for everything we like to eat, and the garden itself better than any market for variety and quantity. It seems we always go overboard, there's enough here to feed a nation, is that what we've got? Tomatoes are coming now, more every day, the ones that we bypassed as green two suns ago are full and red and torrid, we've luckily thought to bring a saltshaker so we can pick them and sprinkle them and eat them whole, allowing the juices to smear our faces and trickle down into our T-shirts and all the way down to our crotches. The kids come here together to sing and make music, they believe that it helps the plants since it helps them and how could we call them wrong, when eggplants and peppers and even melons will burst from this soil, which is supposed to be Northern and hard?

The garden is where I first took Little-one to lie with me, though mosquitoes covered our bodies and the brown earth clinging to every crevice on our skin like rivers on a map, we rolled and pumped and made the great secrets revealed for a while, in the garden. It is where long afternoon is most striking, it is church, it is synagogue, it is peace on earth and plenty, without it nothing could be. We are never higher or nobler than when we are weeding the eggplants, and all concern for literature and society disappears there in our greater concern for life. Ramrod who speaks the least, who finds it the hardest to put his concerns in words, spends most of his time here. He talks like an ear of corn: ripe and fleshy with positive energy.

After mulching and weeding two-and-a-half rows of potatoes, we are reluctantly leaving the crops for the beaver pond; we could stay with them till sundown, but the sweat on our chests and the slowness of living has convinced us to take a cool refresher. We'll leave Ramrod behind with the cukes and pass under the apple trees—where Mother is annually queen of the appletime, pulled on a cart by me on the tractor, smiling and waving at imaginary bystanders—and onto the road again. The pond is through the deepest woods, two miles from the farm, it is the only clearing in the forest, cold and clear at all seasons except in a drought. The beavers who tend it are fully visible at twilight, propelling themselves around the dam with their tails and picking up sticks for their fire, building their house, raising their family. We swim in the nude as children have done since before the great shame began. We have nothing to hide. It is inconceivably unnatural to live in a family whose members never see each other entirely, the ban which the genital clothing imposes leaves forever a question in their minds, and the family cannot be together. Sometimes I even find strong physical attraction to my brothers and sisters, and I am glad of it.

So, in the waning hours of sunlight, we'll strip to the soul and join the others in paddling across the pond to the improvised stool in the center, an old board nailed on two stumps. Now the water has covered us whole, though we inched our way in, toes to knees to mysterious centers. One by one, the kids from the farm are appearing to swim, they tell of amazing adventures: how the voices of death spoke from the pine grove, a band of gypsies came to the house with fiddles and skirts and tambourines, the clouds rolled over one side of the field and it snowed for a moment in brilliant sunshine, a shooting star was observed, the cow had suddenly and without warning dropped a heifer, who will be raised to a bull, there is raspberry-cream-pie for dessert, the neighboring farm has been sold to a tarot-card reader who also welds Volkswagens with a torch, Mark played the organ into the bright green valley and watched the eternal twilight begin while Bokonon took his own life, and the first of the peaches is ready. They tell all these stories as they circle the pond, gasping for air and spurting out water they might have swallowed but didn't. An old rubber inner tube is supporting Tricky Dick, who smiles easy into the sunset, which goes on in these days for hours and hours, only his browned shoulders and bony legs appearing above the surface of the water. And Jeannie, who so nearly drowned, is sticking to a rubber raft, on which she floats prostrate as a queen of the Nile. It is the witching hour of day, the moments before darkness when the earth is yet warm and fecund, and anything is possible. This is the time when Mother Honeywell is most powerful.

Let me tell you a little about her. This is all a true story. She lived in the days before General Washington, when natives continued to thrive in this place and the families who lived here were together in a religious movement aimed at: apocalypse. By the turn of the nineteenth century (Minus Two Hundred), she and a fellow named Sart proclaimed the world as they knew it would end. On the darkest days of December, before the century turned, they made themselves homes in the highest limbs of the trees, convinced that the further they got toward heaven the better their chance of survival, and wishing at any rate to be the first in the world to see God when He came. After that year, history records nothing of them, books and journals and serial-histories cease. Mother Honeywell and her friends also danced naked in moonlight and swam in this pond. The history of the place, published in town, makes her a superstitious fool on the hill, but with just a typographical shudder of fear. In addition to Sart, she had for a neighbor the only African man on the continent, who called himself 'Bijah; he too was a part of the coven; and his daughter wrote poems published in New York and his son, it is said, could play any musical instrument upon first picking it up. The children of town made up a song about his grave, which if you went there between midnight and dawn, you'd get boogered. The grave is invisible now, buried under by years of trodding on the planet, its stone indistinguishable from the hard earth on which we stand (the clubhouse, for instance, is built on a massive ledge, clearly visible in our basement where Jesse the furnace pulsates and throbs with heat in winter), but I know where it is because I've been boogered. It was a Warm evening not unlike this one, and when 'Bijah came over me, senses and soul, I was lucky indeed to make it back home in one peace.

Anyway Mother Honeywell had two special tricks which she played on the unsuspecting. Neither could cause them real harm. When her shoulder hurt (she had a bit of arthritis), as before a big rain, oxcarts all over town would stop: their left rear wheels blocked by a fieldmouse. And when she was feeling better, people all over the area would find themselves buried under a load of fish: which fell from the sky. She works best when the universe is just getting dark.

I remember my first encounter with her was on Hallowe'en, which follows the end of Warm and precedes the blackness and stillness of winter. Michael and Ramrod and I had been down to the town buying an ancient tractor on payments-of-time, and we drove it home by the brook. All of an instant, the left rear wheel stopped moving, while the right one quickly circled around and the tractor veered sharply into a tree and hung over the darting water, Michael in shock and the machine in a wreck. Old Farmer Ripley came in the morning and fixed it, and the story had a happy ending: to the point of the mailman, Old Bull Lee, coming down with a load of flounder: but somebody burned down the covered bridge at the Pumping Station that night, and the stream there has been impassable ever since.

My second experience in winter: The Lady from Oklahoma and I had been driving a car from a clubhouse down in the South. When we got to the apple tree we considered leaving the vehicle and climbing the hill on our feet, for the snow was flying like faerydust and the land slippery and wet, and the night was coming on. Black Irish, a neighboring grownup, came by in his truck and smiling said put-on-your-chains-you'll-make-it-easy. But alongside the graveyard the left rear wheel of the car stopped abruptly. I got out and saw that the chain had vanished, and was neither wrapped around the axle nor visible in the snow. We walked the rest of the way (Lady from O stopping to piss on a birch in her crouching familiar unpretentious and imprudent way) and got Ed with his jeep to come and tow the unfortunate Volkswagen oxcart. But before he could do so, as he was tugging the half-chained bug, his lights flickered and died. All winter, snow and darkness now—like the time Tricky Dick had to sit out a storm in the hollow of an oak all night in the wrathful elements. With the aid of a flashlight we inched the jeep down the mountain and waited for Michael to come in the Packard—which once took Florenz Ziegfeld to lunch with Myrna Loy. When he arrived and heard of the problems, the Packard's lights too dimmed and died in the storm. Once again Farmer Ripley fixed it all up— "This will do you till morning," he said, affixing a battery-run light to the jeep while his children, all 12 of them, stood in a row from smallest to largest, each holding a tool. "I could eat the asshole right out of a skunk," Ripley concluded. And when we finally got back to the house, Ed's wife Evie announced that for dinner we'd dine upon trout!

And a final example: from the night the children all nearly burned, like their neighboring orphans. The chimney caught fire and threatened to end the adventure. But Ripley's son Timothy happened along on a horse (it was sundown), and knowing of dangers in country living, he showed us how to extinguish the blaze. Later, in the kitchen steaming with scallops and clams brought that day from the ocean, I cursed the good witch who has lived here forever, and continues to influence our lives. And Timothy shunned me in horror, saying as how she who makes these things happen is directly related to the Ripleys as ancestor, and spoke of how they respect her.

But the point to remember is that mischief as she might, Mother Honeywell cannot destroy us; she did not even destroy herself, and lives on in us. Like the time Bokonon's candles burned down my bedpost and set fire to my sleep, and Barf-Barf the missing border collie woke me at dawn saying "Pan, it will soon be too late." We always seem to survive as long as we stay on Total Loss Farm.

Anyway, while the children swim in the beaver pond, fresh and cold and larger than ever after yesterday's rain, a loose wind comes bellowing through the woods. It is a sound they have heard before, the moment before they got lost. It says:

> Winds of Change to Get You
> Yet You
> Will Live Beyond.

It means we are going to die on Total Loss Farm, we will die very soon with the rest of the race, and yet live here forever. That is how we survive, in our souls, and in the beauty in earthly nature which seizes our bodies for organic waste.

And the beaver pond itself grows larger and larger, until we become alarmed. Water is rushing into it from all sides as the sun declines behind the firs and sits now purple and red on the top of the highest western mountain. Nothing stops the wind. Sunset, goodbye to my Lord, come again morning, how it goes on and on. It is the holiest and scariest moment of all: the two minutes before sleep. The reality of our situation has become all too clear. The ocean is coming to get us, the water level is rising, and we paddle and stroke all the way to the borders of the farm, where dry land once again rises, and prepare to be washed away in the flood. But as the sun moves behind the horizon, and the full moon rises now bright and yellow like peaches behind the orchard, it is suddenly apparent what has happened: the ocean has stopped at the edge of the farm, we are all at once an island, it was all downhill from here and now the water has stopped just short of our altitude, we are still on top of it, our noses and mouths in the air so to speak while millions are already drowned. All we must do now to survive is stay as high as we are, or get higher.

It is Mother Honeywell's famous old trick, bringing us within a breath of disaster, then holding us aloft till the morning, when the spell will be broken. This is surely a close one. In the meantime the waters are stilled and fishes are floating ashore, to feed us and keep us through the night, and Silent is making a boat. Total Loss Farm has become the final inhabitable earth on the planet that we are capable of seeing; beyond it, in any direction, just the great waters: except of course for the mountains far off in the west, which are higher yet than we and covered with snow even in Warm. The boat will be made of maple, with elm for joists and supports, and wrapped all around with birchbark. It is big enough for only a few of us to cross the great waters, but those who stay behind will be safe and warm and fed of their own devices until we return. If there is life on our island, in spite of the terrible flood which has killed off so many on lower levels, then there must be other islands, too, where children are playing at mermaids and waiting out the apocalypse on the highest limbs of the trees. They may never be heard from again, but they are alive in the middle of all death, believe me; they are waiting to hear from you, they are hoping against all factual evidence that you, too, are OK after the deluge. And Silent says we must build the boat, though it take all night, and cross the great waters in it, to know for sure that we are not alone, to bring the spirit of Total Loss Farm to the ends of the dying planet. We will leave in the hours before dawn, and be back when the sun has crested the barn and the crops and animals and people once again spreading their love on the land.

We will paddle our boat across the great waters looking for what we have just left behind, looking for the farm and whatever survivors may be yet swimming about in circles over the waterlogged cities, hoping to be rescued. There is no need to worry about us: we will make it across and back again, getting from nowhere to nowhere, and go on living in love and our sins on Total Loss Farm forever. They told us the planet was going away, that soon it would not support life: those are the facts. But the children say, "facts are always the same, the end has been coming since the beginning, we've known it since we were born. Facts are not interesting to us any more. Those who will make it are those who want to. The others, having lost faith, are as good as drowned already in their salty tears for the past." They propose to make it on the strength of love alone, as love is all they have left, and are grateful to be living in the era during which love has been put to its finest and greatest test.

There is no adventure greater than ours. We are the last life on the planet, it is for us to launch the New Age, to grow up to be *men* and *women* of earth, and free of the walking dead who precede us. To make it to morning. We will need to be so together that impartial observers could never tell us apart: "they all look the same to me." We have no money or guns, but we have a piece of the earth which is yet tonight as it was meant to be, alive and exploding with mystery. From where we are, you might look to the stars and the heavens or straight down into the dirt, where a million tiny miracles are taking place under your nose: and see in either a dazzling timeless store of energy. We are a part of it.

The boat is nearing completion, and the dawn cannot be far away, for the sparrows and chickadees are now punctuating the darkness with song. It will be another warm day when it comes, the fog will be burned out and the ocean recede under the strength of the sun. The farm will go on making food, animals running around the barn, and people too giving new life, babies coming into the picture all over and taking their places among us. How can we ever believe that all this could cease to be? We will never believe it. Instead we are sailing the ocean and smiling at daybreak and eagerly pushing toward the morning ahead, when words will be forgotten, when only the song of the totality and our mutual loving vibration will be heard on the earth. We are young, and did not create the poisons which have already killed our parents and do not indulge in them. We are young, and demand the right to live and to love each other, and to play on the gorgeous incredible planet. We expect to be smothered with kindness wherever we go, for what else would make sense in a world so close to the end? We intend to cooperate. We are coming to get you, over the waters, in our homespun craft, we hope you'll be ready to go when we get there. To go to the farm in time for sunrise in Warm.

All the children will be sleeping when the sun comes back. They will rise to the sounds of birds and peepfrogs and Taj the rooster who will always and ever crow at the dawn. The eastern horizon will move from black to lurid blue until a faint red streak at its root becomes flaming crimson. It will happen again and again. It will never stop happening before us until we are one with it, no longer making it happen but doing it for ourselves.

Good morning, Henry Thoreau, good morning me, good morning you. Good morning, good morning, good morning. In my dim recall of yesterday, the beaver pond rose till we stood apart and alone on the planet, Silent's boat shoved off on the waters and we wondered who among all those millions would make it with us to the dawn.

Mark has been making a creakity wooden sign saying "Total Loss Farm" so they'll know the place when they get here. My arms and legs and kidneys and heart are yet moving, I am yet carrying myself outside to look to the east and sing to the sun. Good morning, good morning, good morning.

—April, 1970

AUTUMN AGAIN:
A Year in the Life

A year turns around in the Life like a vast and weighty rhythm, slow and laboring it goes on and on until it is done, yet it grows briefer and simpler the further behind us it falls. A year is the perfect measure of time, for it brings all things full circle. What was before, is now. Who was living is now dying, who was dead now resurrected. Autumn in particular is the time for dying, yet it puts on such a good show of it that nobody really minds—until of course it is too late, and the cold sets in. But it is autumn, not posthumous winter, which is really the end.

Since we always think of ourselves as greatly changed with each year, advancing you might say on some kind of head development which will not end, it is helpful to be able to think that each year grows truer and better than the last. Of course it all depends on how you look at it; the word "optimist" literally means the one who *sees best*. I believe that most Lifers are optimists. They are the ones, at any rate, who have not yet given up.

October makes the planet so bright and crisp it seems like another world, something we have dreamed, an ecstasy so great that it could not happen on earth, at least not for long. And October and autumn, like spring, is brief. While it lasts, it is our most daring flirtation with disaster.

Disaster is everywhere visible, even without straining your eyes too much, and that is one of the things which makes optimism so difficult. We have our moments of inconsolable grief, and some of actually waging war against ourselves—but more and more, don't you think, we're learning how to be higher and wider? The city grows ever closer to the country, but the opposite is also true. More and more we are fewer and fewer, and someday we will be One—or None. Both are fine numbers to be once you're there, but when you're still trying to *make it* things can be tough. We're doing our best, though. My brothers are dying of junk and jail, we must show them a better way.

The houses that burn will be replaced, the folks who die will be reincarnated—as people, perhaps, or just blades of grass—the forces of repressive technology and behavior will grow weaker and less awesome the more people lose fear of them. The sun will rise and set until it doesn't. We will always be an insignificant portion of the energy in the air, yet perfectly tuned as a vital part of a perfect system. Yes it is good, it is everything, we cannot question its morality. Yes it is good. Keep your eye on the sky.

So the years go, always in upheaval until we nearly think we understand what it is to die and have lost our fear even of that. Beyond that we are free. Freedom has been the word all along: perhaps we secretly know that we will never get there, but it certainly is fun to play at getting closer. Freedom means you never feel bad about something you really have to do, you never do anything bad. We are asking for the sky, no? Not satisfied even with still having the earth, we demand the clouds and air as well—and water—and trees—and dogs—and quivering mountains. We want the right to take them for granted. We demand space, outer and inner.

We are demanding it of ourselves, not of society or the nation or any other such abstractions: we are striving to be so real.

It gets to the point where you start thinking the spot you are standing on is intimately related to China, since you could just walk and row in the right direction and the very earth would carry you there.

We are going to make it, believe me and it will be true. We will do all the shit we have to do to make it true. We will just give up everything and only do nice things. Do you doubt it? Doubt then tomorrow. And tomorrow is a whole new ballgame.

Hang on, dear friend. The greatest show on earth goes on. Ain't seen nothing yet. How could I not have *realized*.

About the Author

Raymond Mungo is a writer of some reputation and very little emotional stability. Far from striving for cool detachment, he seems always to be overreacting to his situation: laughing, crying, being hauled off by the police, fervently speaking to trees, changing his mind. He was born in 1946, Pisces, Scorpio rising. He did a lot of political stuff. Now he lives with these twelve other people on some farm up in Vermont, but sometimes he goes to Peru, at least in his head. He is just trying to make it, same as everybody.

—Abraham Mazo